CHRIST'S GRACE & BAPTISM MENU:
50 DAYS OF DAILY MANNA BAPTISM & GRACE
BY JJ BOTHA

CHRIST'S GRACE & BAPTISM MENU:
50 Days of Daily Manna Baptism & Grace
Author: Jacobus JJ Botha,

Published By Parables
September, 2018

All Rights Reserved. No part of this book may be reproduced or utilized in any form or by any means, electronic or mechanical, including photocopying, recording, or by any information storage and retrieval system, without permission in writing from the author.

    ISBN 978-1-945698-73-6
    Printed in the United States of America

Readers should be aware that Internet Web sites offered as citations and/or sources for further information may have been changed or disappeared between the time this was written and the time it is read.

CHRIST'S GRACE & BAPTISM MENU:
50 DAYS OF DAILY MANNA BAPTISM & GRACE
BY JJ BOTHA

PUBLISHED by PARABLES
Earthly Stories with a Heavenly Meaning

Chapter 1
FUNDAMENTAL DOCTRINE

Matthew 7: 13- 14 Enter ye in at the strait gate, for wide is the gate, and broad is the way that leadeth to destruction, and many there be which go in there at; Because strait is the gate, and narrow is the way, which leadeth unto life, and few there be that find it.

The Christian faith is about salvation and eternal life in Christ, yet these things are not the primary concerns of many converts these last days. Maybe because of anxieties, worries, and troubles of this life; I don't know what other preachers think or have to say about church and salvation in this new age. It is obvious the comforts of this life and values of this sinful world are actually taking over the place of salvation in the hearts

CHRIST'S GRACE & BAPTISM
MENU:
50 DAYS OF DAILY MANNA
BAPTISM & GRACE
BY
JJ BOTHA

THE COVER OF THIS BOOK EXPLAINED:

On this picture, you will see the Word as a sharp two-edged Sword (with its handle in Heaven) in the center of the Bible. This Sword cuts and brings division on earth between soul and spirit, between joint and marrow (like a healing blade during a delicate operation) and exposes our innermost thoughts and desires. You will see the Bible as the inspired Scripture that must be opened to tell you about the Word or about Jesus Christ the Lord as Person. He forms the center of the Bible (and in this picture). It is all about His death on our behalf and our resurrection with Him. See the open Bible. See the Living Waters flowing in and from it (blue). The Whole Bible is about the crucifixion of Jesus our Savior and the resurrection of Christ Jesus our Lord. Can you see the cross through which He died? Can you see the hurt in that cross, and the crown of thorns that resembled that pain? The cross is the sword that looks dull in our fleshly realm, but the sharp sword in His hands in the spirit realm that divided history in an Old Testament and a New Testament. First a dark period of law and then a period of Light and Grace etc. (like explained in "The Unintended Book of Grace"). He rose from the water grave or came to Life when the Spirit of God descended like a Dove, raised Him from that death at Calvary and declared Him as the Eternal Truth or Word of Truth that cannot die or ever be buried or ever be ignored! No, eventually the Truth will stand up in you! You will proclaim Him. You will become bold. The Lion of Truth Himself will speak and roar through you. See the water and blood (drops) that speaks of death, but also of birth. Please see: "For there are three who bear witness, the Spirit, and the water, and the blood: and the three agree in One (1 John 5:8, ASV)." See how all this can be seen in the open Scripture only. All those pages in the Bible around Him represents the same message that we all must listen to on earth. That Message comes from Heaven. See the pages on top of Him as Heaven proclaiming this Message of Truth to us in this picture. Those pages represent us as part of the Living Word and the cloud of witnesses. We are all part of the Living Truth. Your life speaks! See the Glory from Heaven (Gold and scarlet). See the open heaven. Too much to mention. One picture really tells a thousand words! This is why God likes to speak to us in pictures, dreams and visions (Rev 1:2).

Christ's Grace And Baptism

Thanks George Maartens for drawing this picture for us by only using coloring pens.

PREFACE

I shared these daily pieces about the water baptism on request of some of my friends on Facebook a few years ago. I copied and pasted it today to form a book and it gives us exactly 50 daily pieces to work through in order to understand some of the meaning of the water baptism.

I have used capital letter words in this small booklet for certain words that are not normally spelled with capital letters. The reason is that it refers to Christ. Therefore, I do it out of respect. It is not by mistake. There is revelation behind it, so please let this not hinder you in your reading of this daily pieces of manna, but rather let it guide you in your Biblical meditations on this subject.

It is important to understand the three dimensions that God works in (in order for our souls to grasp what already happened in spirit at Calvary). It is important to maybe first read: "The Unintended Book of Grace" to grasp the foundational truths about "Christ in us" before reading this booklet. In any case, may the reading of this book be a blessing to you, may it give you light and increase the richness in revelation that you already cherish about the content and meaning of the baptism. May the wisdom of God as partly portrayed in the meaning of the Baptism, overwhelm you, increase your adoration for Christ and may your gratitude towards our Father be bigger than you ever imagined and become a constant worship on your lips!

"Brothers and sisters, think of what you were when you were called. Not many of you were wise by human standards; not many were influential; not many were of noble birth. But God chose the foolish things of the world to shame the wise; God chose the weak things of the world to shame the strong" (1 Cor. 1:26, 27, NIV). This is so 100 % applicable to myself! I have absolutely nothing to boast in. My faith is so weak. Most of the time I simply do not know what God wants me to do next. I know our lives are in His hands, but maybe we have too many toys and things to worry about when He wants us to move? Sometimes I know His will for now, but I want to know His plans for us for the future. This is where my problem comes from. I want to walk where I can see and not where He sees (and I cannot). This is especially true if His guidance does not make any financial sense. Some people mistakenly called me a man of faith, but they do not know my doubts and fears at times of trouble and when taking a step in the dark is required. Then I often behave like *Simon-Simon* the reed blown hither and thither - instead of standing steadfast in my faith like a rock. Do not let me fool you with a masquerade of faith or sounding as if "I arrived" (if I cannot put my money where my mouth is).

I now think of a situation when God gave me a job in George in South Africa. I greeted my friends and went there full of faith. I strongly believed it was from God. Things did not immediately work out the way I wanted it to. I jumped back to the known comfort zone of my familiar environment. I took the first steps, but never pushed through. Fear and panic overwhelmed me and withheld me from pushing through. I was so happy to be back in my known comfort zone, but I later regret not trusting God all the way (because then it was clear to see that I should have trusted Him all the way). The fact that I did not push through prevented me from entering the bigger blessing God had in store for me. He was unable to do many miracles there because of their disbelief (Mat 13:58, CEB). I often see this kind of struggles and unbelief in other people's lives as well (I am like the person who sees the splinter in other peoples' eyes...). I can see how people start in faith and then jump back or run back to their known familiar environment. They then thank God for just being safely back in the old comfort zone (like I did, but I missed the thing God planned for me – just as they do). Even this is good and acceptable to God. He will comfort me and not love me less if I just want to anchor myself in the known, but how can you know what is on the other side if you do not push through? (Moreover, I mean all the way until the very end!).

If you really want to grow in faith and trust in Him, He will again teach you how to fly and again test your flying skills on another occasion. You might fall again, but as the Mighty Eagle He is, He will carry you back to safety until He knows you are right to rewrite the test all over again! What if the road is tough and harder than you imagined? What if it takes so much longer than you imagined? What if it is difficult to hear God's voice when the dark waves roar in all the turmoil around you? What if the storm threatens to demolish you? What if fear is almost unavoidable? What if the reward is bigger than you imagined? What if God wants to take you through trials like Job experienced? What if you also feel like coming to the end of yourself just like Job did? What if you really lose everything and really come to the end of yourself as Job did? Moses had faith to cross the desert on his own, but guiding all those people through the desert was a different story! Moses guided more than 2 million people through the desert. That is faith! How can God do miracles if I do not believe? The father instantly cried out, "I do believe, but help me overcome my unbelief!" (Mark 9:24, NLT). How I must cry out to God tonight!

Still I wrote this book, my beloved friend. I still want you to read it, in spite of my own weaknesses and weakness! I am so weak, but the Word is alive, mighty, powerful and He brings division between that which originated in our heads or imagination and that, which comes from Him. So, please read everything even though it might be controversial. Scripture always interpret Scripture in the end. There are many other Scriptures in the Bible that I cannot share with you, as I am too dumb to understand it out of myself. My own vision is excessively limited. I will probably stay blind to many portions, until the day that God will open it for me and then I would like to share it with you as well. Off course, you are free to differ from what I have written in this small booklet. I am open and look forward to repent where I have quoted a certain verse or piece of Scripture out of context. Repentance always means growth and better understanding for me. So please, before you just disregard this content, please ask yourself: "Is it possible for God to speak through a normal inconspicuous fisherman?" If it is possible for God, please just go and look at these daily pieces and the Scripture quoted. If portions are maybe against your traditional dogmas, then believe Scripture in spite of what I have written or the traditions of man might have taught you.

A Man with a sword in His Hand (or Mouth - Rev 1:16) appeared to Joshua. Joshua asked Him: ""Are you for us or for our enemies (Josh 5:13-15, NIV)?" The MAN definitely did not associate Himself with our thinking patterns like: "Are you for the Reformed people or for the Pentecostal people or with which denomination do you associate yourself with?" No! The cross of

Jesus already eliminated all division between people. Only lies, denominationalism and theology still separate us in our fleshly pride. Our Father is interested in you following His Word or His Son as a Person. Christ is one billion times more important than the rules and dogma that some people rely on. Dogmas and religion divides, but Love (He) unites. That is why He died on that cross. The choice to follow the Word is always in our own hands. The Man answered Joshua: "I have come now as captain of the army of the Lord." Then Joshua fell with his face toward the earth and bowed down, and said to him, "What does my lord have to say to his servant (Josh 5:14, Amplified)?" "The captain of the Lord's army said to Joshua, 'Remove your sandals from your feet, because the place where you are standing is holy (set apart to the Lord)' (Josh 5:15)."

I believe God has something to say to us. I believe we can stand on holy ground if we are humble enough to listen and learn.

DEDICATION:

I dedicate this book to the daughter that I love: "Talitha".

I want to encourage you with this book, Talitha my daughter. Thank you for recently surrendering your life to Christ. We prayed for that for so long. Remember, in the end your relationship with God is the only thing that really matters. Everything else is temporary.

It was your recent curiosity about the baptism that motivated me to publish this daily pieces (in which I discussed the water baptism), in order for other people to also know and see what we see, know and cherish. May you radically pursue His presence and daily desire God with all in you!

May your life have purpose and a bigger meaning to daily pursue in Christ!

Day 1 Why talk about baptism?

    I grew up with a certain paradigm about baptism. I embraced the tradition that my ancestors followed. I promised Carien two things after I was born again. One thing was that I would never be "baptized for a second time". I believed that I was already baptized as a baby. One night I dreamed about Noah. I was with Noah and his family in the ark. I could literally see and experience the flood. The next morning I felt in my spirit that God wanted me to be baptized, but I rejected the idea due to my promise to Carien. "Baptism cannot save anybody!" I told myself. Baptism was not an important thing in my eyes then and I still do not want to make it a bigger thing than just to give it the place that it deserves according to Scripture. God became quiet in my life after that. I did not know what was wrong. I vigorously defended the traditional baptism that I knew. I used intense arguments on several occasions (some of my readers can testify about that).

    One day God told me that I was like steel in His hands in my own pride. He said that He could not bend, form and mould me, because I am not clay in the hands of the Potter. Immediately I knew He was talking about the baptism issue. I was a bit surprised, because I decided on only two small things that I was not willing to test against Scripture, surrender in His hands and ask for His guidance. I then realized that deep inside me I was afraid. I was afraid that my beliefs and doctrines that I so desperately clang to and defended with my life could be wrong. If I were wrong, it would mean that I would have to admit it. That part really scared my pride or ego. What would the people say, especially because I so aggressively defended and proclaimed my doctrinal believes in which I grew up?

    I finally spoke to God and asked Him to reveal His will to me. Then God gave me the same dream. For a second time I was with Noah and his family in the ark. I could literally see the turmoil and the dirty masses of water that took the godless away. It was so clear, so real and so frightening to experience it in my spirit. It was the first time ever in my life as far as I can remember that I dreamed the same dream twice (at that stage). It was supernatural to me. That morning God confirmed my dream by giving me Scripture out of the book of Peter. I humbly want to share it with you.

Please, my purpose is not to try and persuade anybody to be baptized, because that would be empty. I just want to help you see the meaning and the power of the water baptism as a mighty weapon for the soul of the Christian. I do not want to make it complicated, but just want to share it with you in the same simplicity that I received it from God. I also beg you in Love to take this issue to God and just test everything to Scripture while praying for the Holy Spirit to open the Scripture to you. I cannot do it. Only God can give us Light. We must never harden our hearts, but rather follow His soft and gentle guidance. May this few pieces that follow bless you and enrich you. May your baptism be a mighty weapon for your soul!

Day 2 Baptism is a weapon for your soul and not for your spirit

Not only had the murderer on the cross, but also thousands of other people received Eternal Life without ever being baptized. Your spirit is not saved through baptism. You can only be saved by receiving the Life of Christ in your spirit or by being born from Above or born from Him (John 1;12, 13, 3:3, 1 Pet 1:23). Peter explains the place of the baptism for us. "Once the patience of God waited in the days of Noah, while the ark was being made ready, wherein few, that is, eight *souls* were saved by water. Unto the figure of which the baptism that does now correspond saves us (not taking away the uncleanness of the flesh, but giving testimony of a good conscience before God) by the resurrection of Jesus, the Christ (1 Pet 3:20-21, JUB)." Make sure you see that it was eight *souls* saved. Your old flesh and sin body already died at the cross when you were born again (you lost the uncleanness of the flesh there during your rebirth). It did not happen during your baptism! No! Your baptism is only a weapon for your *head* or *soul* or *mind* or *thoughts* to cling to in order to remind you about what really happened at that cross when you got born again or born from Above or born out of God. Your whole fight on this earth is in your *soul*. The whole onslaught of the enemy and the evil forces are aimed against *your thoughts* and your mind. Your spirit is above this turmoil and rests with God in heavenly places. This is why Peter said only two verses further (from the quoted portion) that we must arm ourselves with this thought that we stopped sinning, because we died to sin according to the flesh (because Jesus died in our place). It is therefore not necessary for any person on earth that armed his mind with this thought to continue sinning while still alive on this earth. We can now rule over sin (1 Pet 4:1, 2). The water baptism is therefore *not* the salvation of the spirit, but *is a weapon to arm the soul* while we are on our road of sanctification. We really trust Our Father to guide us while looking deeper into this.

Please just continue to read. Do not think and tell people that we never sin. No, we rule over sin. It is not that we do not ever falter and never make mistakes. No, it is just that it is now the exception. If we accidentally stumble, we know that He already died for that (like explained in the Unintended Book of Grace).

Grace is never a license for sinning, but He empowers us with His Life in order to reign over it.

Day 3 The baptism of the earth during Noah's flood

"There is one body and one Spirit, just as you were called to one hope when you were called; one Lord, one faith, one baptism; one God and Father of all, who is over all and through all and in all (Eph 4:4-6, BSB)." After I read this, I realised that if God says "one", then there cannot be two or more different baptisms and both from Him. I prayed and begged Him to show me the real so that I could identify the fake or counterfeit and the imitations from the enemy. Then God linked my dream of Noah with baptism and it all fell in place for me. He guided me through His Holy Spirit to see that the flood in Noah's time was a pure reflection, image or explanation for us in order to understand baptism.

"Once the patience of God waited in the days of Noah, while the ark was being made ready, wherein few, that is, *eight souls* were saved by water. Unto the figure of which the baptism that does now correspond saves us (not taking away the uncleanness of the flesh, but giving testimony of a good conscience before God) by the resurrection of Jesus, the Christ (1 Pet 3:20-21, JUB)." I read this passage and then went to the OT while meditating on it. I saw that the earth was bad and polluted with sin according to Scripture. I read how God sent a mighty flood. "Finally, the mighty flood was so deep that even the highest mountain peaks were almost twenty-five feet below the surface of the water (Gen 7:20, CEV)." When I read that, it was as if God Himself said to me: "Do not let anybody tell you that the flood covered only a part of the earth". That is just pure intellectual reasoning without reading Scripture or believing Genesis 8:9.

God showed me how He baptized the earth. It happened in the days of Noah. A big flood of water that covered the earth and that will never ever be repeated. It was a perfect image of baptism. The water saved Noah and his family, because the earth was cleaned from the giants by the flood, the demonic creatures of Genesis 6:4 and the demonic oppression of that time. The earth was different after it was baptized and after it emerged out of the water. This is the first idea or thought that you must cherish according to Peter and the history of Noah. Is it not beautiful? We were like the old earth (same minerals in our bodies) and part of the old earth in ourselves before the cross, but after the cross, we are now new creations or totally new creatures. We now stand before Him perfected by His blood. We are already part of His Kingdom and already part of the new earth that will soon manifest.

Day 4 Only One Branch after the death during the flood

God showed us how the whole earth was completely covered or submerged under water (Gen 7:19). The dove that Noah sent out (a shadow type of the Holy Spirit), confirmed this. The dove returned without any life (Gen 8:9). Everything was dead as confirmed by the dove ("Holy Spirit"). Exactly like God said it would be (Gen 6:13). Isaiah saw exactly the same thing during his prophetic vision of the cross. Isaiah saw that all "plants" (us – nations – earthly people) were dead after the cross. There was absolutely no growth or any life on earth that he could see (Is 10:23, 25, 33-34). Noah indirectly saw the cross and the total destruction brought by it during the flood. "...we are convinced that One died for all, therefore all died (2 Cor 5:14, BSB). Nothing of the old remained alive due to the flood. Nothing of Adam remained due to the cross. Adam was finished. It is finish. Just death! Just disaster! Nothing of the old remained.

Then the Holy Spirit brought the good news. "The dove came back to him in the evening, grasping a torn olive leaf in its beak. Then Noah knew that the waters were subsiding from the earth (Gen 8:11, CEB)."

The moment Noah saw the Olive Leaf, He saw the Shoot or the Branch out of the stem of Jesse that would bear His fruit on earth (Is 11:1). The Dove had to open his eyes to see that death is not the end. No, death cannot ever be victorious. Noah realised and he knew there was/is no life possible without it coming from the Root of Jesse.

Peter said that *baptism is a prayer to God* (1 Pet 3:21). See your Creator and Father during this sacrament of baptism. See the Life that is before all Creation or before all other life. He is the Alpha! The Holy Spirit wants us to turn our focus on Him. He is before all. He is the only Branch or Root with Life on the other side of the cross (Is 11:1). There is nothing on the other side of the cross that did not come out of Him, that is not from Him and is not in Him! Absolutely nothing. Everything united through His cross.

We worship you Holy God! We want to honour the intention of the Holy Spirit and only focus on You. You are the One and only Guarantee that we have for the glorification of our bodies and the new earth. Holy Spirit, please continue to place our focus on Christ. When we do focus like you want us to focus, o

God, we know (just like Noah when he focused away from the subsiding water around him and on the Shoot) that the new earth will soon emerge (Selah)!

Day 5 We came out of "One Ark with Three Storeys"

God told Noah precisely how to build the ark. "You shall make it with lower, second, and third stories (Gen 6:16, TLV)."

The fullness of something is always expressed in all three dimensions. We get the positive degree, then the comparative degree and then the superlative degree. Love has length, breadth and height (or depth). Worldly people can walk in the two horizontal dimensions of Love (length and breadth). They can know fleshly love and soul love, but they can never know the Height, enter the Depth of God, or touch the Spirit. How sorry I feel for the shallow life of the poor atheist.

The temple or the tabernacle was divided in the forecourt, the holy part and the holy of holies. When people entered the temple in the OT, they entered a certain dimension of the presence of God. When Noah and his family entered the ark, they entered the temple and the presence of God. Noah entered one temple, but he also entered three divisions. One ark, three divisions. In Him they lived and moved, found their security and had their existence (Acts 17:28). One Holy Spirit God. One Father, Son and Holy Spirit. He is our Father in spirit, our oldest Brother in flesh: "The Firstborn of all creation (Col 1:15)."

God demonstrated man's origin to him in the baptism of Noah. There was nothing during the flood (Gen 6:17). All that now live and move on earth came out of Him just like the people and animals came out of that ark (Gen 8:19). "Through Him all things were made, and without Him nothing was made that has been made (John 1:3, BSB)." If we can go back in time, we will only see the ark on the water. Just the Ark (Gen 1:2). If we can go further back in time, we will only see the Word (John 1:1). We (you and me) were in Him. See the origin of all animal and human life that came out of that ark in your mind. This will help you to see how all was in the Word. Faith is to understand that He spoke and then it came into being in the seen realm (Heb 11:3). Our baptism reminds us of this Truth and Objective Reality!

Jacobus JJ Botha

Day 6 The Way through the water is only available to believers!

    I can still remember how I prayed about the passage that compared the flood of Noah with our own water baptism. I was so excited when God showed me how the earth was once totally baptized or completely submerged under water and never again (because the rainbow or the sign of the Reign of Peace followed prophetically after that - *Selah*).

    Then the Holy Spirit showed me a next thing. He showed me that Noah and his family believed in God, while not a single other family on earth did. "And he didn't spare the ancient world when he brought a flood on the world of ungodly people, even though he protected Noah, a preacher of righteousness, along with seven others (2 Pet 2:5, CEB)."

    God saved Noah. On the one hand, there were the ungodly people who could not go through the division of water that separated the old earth and the new earth. On the other hand, there were the eight believers who could experience the new and deeper walk in Christ and the other side of the flood. I was so excited. God showed me that the "Way" through the water was only for believers. No unbeliever can ever pass through the water. It is an exclusive Way that God provides for His children only. We are so fortunate to be His children.

    God is only a Father. It is not biblical to portray Him as a "grandfather" or as an "uncle". If Scripture does not support a certain doctrine, then we must know it is unscriptural and repent from it or turn our backs on it and follow the guidance of the Word.

    "You have come to the meeting of God's firstborn children. Their names are written in heaven. You have come to God, the judge of all people. And you have come to the spirits of good people who have been made perfect (Heb 12:23, ERV)."

    We all are first born and original children of our Father the Father of our spirits inside our bodies. I do not automatically belong to Him just because my dad or granddad did. I testified in "The Unintended book of Grace" how I almost end up in hell believing such a lie until our Father miraculously saved me. You can never boast or count on such a doctrine (Jer 9:24, 1 Cor 1:31, 2 Cor 10:17, Gal 6:14). No! You must have your own personal relationship with Christ Jesus our Lord. The Unique Way that God provided is not available to people who love the present world (except if they stop despising Christ and His cross, repent and turn to our Saviour God).

We as believers now stand on the other side of the water. I cannot go back to the old (because of the separation of water between the old and me). I am part of the new earth. I am a new creation in the Kingdom of our Father who is also the Only King of Heaven or the spirit world. There is only a "now" or a present and a Great Future for me (I have no past on this side of the water)!

Day 7 It was by faith that the people crossed the Red Sea – Heb 11:29

The Israelites were only freed from Egypt when they associated themselves with the blood of the Lamb that was slaughtered for them (Ex 12). Without the blood of the Lamb, it would not have been possible for them to leave Egypt. The blood of the Lamb always changes us from slaves of religion to free people that can leave Egypt and its slavery behind and follow Christ the King in the freedom of Grace. We can live because the Only begotten Son of God or "the Only-born from the Father (John 1:14, DLNT)", became the *Firstborn among many brethren* (Rom 8:29, Col 1:15, 18). Christ died for all of us who are firstborn children and for those that will still be part of the firstborn (Ex 12:27). The different images that God uses are always perfect (like biblical marriage between a man and a woman as an example of our relationship with Him). So remember, it is first the blood of the Lamb and then you will taste the freedom of leaving Egypt. God showed me that there was a struggle between His children and Pharaoh (because Pharaoh wanted – and still wants - to keep God's children under yokes or religious yokes). It costed our Redeemer His earthly Life, His *soul*; His precious blood in order to free us from the enemy's control (Is 53:10). Only after the children of God turned their backs on Egypt, could they cut the soul ties they had with Egypt. How? By their baptism. By also crossing the furthest borders of the enemies control in the experiential realm. The children of God could see and experience the end of the enemy and his reign over them (when the enemy drowned by the flood God used). Can you see that this way of saving the soul of the believer is only available to them that already turned their backs on Egypt (1 Pet 3:20). The Holy Spirit only guided the people that already turned their backs on Pharaoh to the water or the final separation between the old and the new. Hebrews 11:27, 28 shows us how the believers could only leave Egypt by Faith. They could only partake of the blood of the Lamb by Faith. "By an act of faith, Israel walked through the Red Sea on dry ground. The Egyptians tried it and drowned (Heb 11:29, MSG)." Can you see that God always confirms His Word? Can you see that it is exactly as it was with Noah? NB: It is essential to believe Scripture and see that they could only cross the Red Sea by Faith. Trying to go through the water without Faith, will produce spiritual death (like with Pharaoh) and legalism or a mind still bound to fear and to the slavery of religion and religious yokes. The separation through water or the way that God made is always *only* available to the *believer*. Paul explained how going through the Red Sea was the baptism of that group of believers who turned their backs on Egypt (1 Cor 10:2). This baptism did not work for the Egyptians.

Day 8 Cut the soul ties and all ties linking you to Egypt!

Whenever a child is born, cut the ties that he or she had with their previous world (the womb, or the old). It is extremely important for that child's survival. Final separation is always necessary. A child cannot continue to live forever with his umbilical cord attached to the old or his previous existence. Even if he still sucks his thumb or still do the things he used to do in his previous world (Ezek 16:4, 9).

After you were born from Above or from the Spirit Father of all spirits, we need to cut the soul ties with Egypt or with our previous existence (so, even if we think that our provision and security is still in this current world and in this current corrupt worldly system, we must break with it).

God knew that Pharaoh and his soldiers would try to again subject us into the slavery of religious works and own plans. This is why God gave us the baptism as an extreme powerful and mighty *weapon for the soul* (1 Cor 10:2). New children of God get the first chance to testify at the water that they must go through in order to sanctify or wash their souls (James 2:14, 17, 22-24). Faith always works like this. Always faith and then the works that flow from it as Scripture explains (never the other way around, because the law could save nobody. If we could do good works that will eventually lead to faith, then Jesus died in vain. The "good works" are still fruit from the wrong tree. The tree of *good* and evil). No! We tapped into God's Faith when we were born from Above. After our union with Him, works of Faith started to flow out of us. Works can never lead to Faith. In fact, if you want to do good works in order to impress God, you will prevent yourself and others from ever obtaining Faith. Only God Himself enables His children to go through the water (1 Pet 3:20).

By going through the water, you can gain the surety in your mind that Pharaoh – as type of Satan – lost his final grip on your life. He will never ever be a factor in your life again.

Baptism is a sacrament. A sacrament is a symbol or physical sign of your own Faith. When you as a believer get baptized, you not only testify about your own personal Faith to both the church and the world around you, but you also proclaim your victory to the spiritual realm and in the face of a "bound in chains" enemy (1 Pet 3:19). We know and with our baptism, we declare by Faith that the enemy fell and that his might is finally and totally broken in our lives. If the defeated enemy still wants to make you believe through his lies that he can continue to be a factor in your life, conquer those evil and lying thoughts (or wrong thought patterns) by thinking of your victory and the enemy's defeat when you passed through that water. Any onslaught from your past can now be defeated by recalling and reliving your baptism in your mind. The baptism confirms that final and permanent division between you and Egypt. You are now free to serve God alone and follow Him in the desert while He daily guides you to the fullness of Christ. Never again will the enemy get any honour for anything positive or negative in your life, simply because he cannot follow you to this side of the water! Your life is in our Fathers hands.

Day 9 Although your stains were like scarlet, you are as white as snow

We must always remember where we came from. Remember that the church even lost the most basic light from Scripture or the most basic foundational truths during the Great Tribulation. The very first Light that broke through the darkness, was when Luther received the revelation that all the millions of dead works and dead religious rituals means absolutely nothing to God. Only Faith in Jesus Christ counts. Only faith in what He accomplished at Calvary. Nothing else can save people. Not even your baptism.

I asked my readers to mark Hebrews 6:1 with a number one in pen. Then God gave more Light to the church. A whole lot of people saw the truth about water baptism, its meaning and its place. This is number 2 that you can mark in your Bible if you want to. "Teaching about baptizing people in water (Heb 6:2, WE)." Most translations talk about baptisms (plural), because there was also the baptism of repentance that John the Baptist used. The people then looked forward to the coming Messiah or the coming Christ during that baptism. Their baptism or the baptism of John the Baptist was different to our own baptism. The baptism of Christ became a reality after the resurrection of Christ and our baptism reminds us that Christ Jesus already paid the price.

John the Baptist was the first person to baptize people. The people in those days knew the habit of "βαπτίζω" or "baptizo". In those days, the people used to take a piece of material and "baptized" it, "dipped" it or "submerged" it into water mixed with colorant. When the material came out on the other side of the water, it was like a total new piece of material. It was like a metamorphosis that the material underwent. It was one colour in the materials' old existence, but it came out on the other side full of beauty, radiant with splendour and like something totally different and new. Just like that, our own water baptism reminds us of what happened to us when we were born again. We were "red people" or full of stains like scarlet (blemished souls) and full of sin and unrighteousness (Matt 5:21, 22, 1 John 3:15), but due to the death of Christ at Calvary, He changed us from the colour of sin (scarlet) to pure white. "The Lord says, 'Now, let's settle the matter. You are stained red with sin, but I will wash you as clean as snow. Although your stains are deep red, you will be as white as wool (Is 1:18, GNT).'"

We do not walk around with the colour of sin or the colour of blood (due to even the most serious offence of murder) on our hands anymore. We are totally new people! We are holy and white as snow due to the cleansing power of the blood of the Lamb!

Day 10 Baptized in the sea – 1 Cor 10:2

"The Red Sea is one of the saltiest bodies of water in the world, owing to high evaporation. Salinity ranges from between 36 % in the southern part because of the effect of the Gulf of Aden water and reaches 41 % in the northern part, owing mainly to the Gulf of Suez water and the high evaporation *(https://en.wikipedia.org/wiki/Red_Sea)*." I only quoted this from google, to show you that the Israelites crossed a salty Red Sea. They crossed the sea once only after leaving Egypt (Scripture already proved that it can never happen the other way around in spite of popular doctrine advocating it. According to Scripture salvation is always first and then sanctification. The spirit is saved first, then the sanctification of the soul follows, and it can never be the other way around – John 3:3). Impossible!

The moment the believers or children of God went through the sea, they were baptized in the sea (1 Cor 10:2). Cling to this sign or image in order to help you with the battle in your mind.

I can remember how my mom used to take meat and then "baptize" it or submerge it in salty water and take it out again after a day or two. The meat will rot if you do not pickle it, but if it was baptized in that salty water or brine, it is preserved from rotting. The bacteria and germs of this world cannot spoil it (compared to the same piece of meat that did not go through the same process). This image of the baptism is to remind us that the cross changed our being or our nature. We are now salted and influenced or preserved by Eternal Life. We are now the salt of this earth and we must preserve the earth with our salt or expand the Kingdom of Christ with the values of the Holy Spirit (Matt 5:13, 13:33). We exchanged our temporary rotten earthly state of existence, which was so entangled in the power and might of sin, for a new preserved and Eternal Life, which is holy.

Do not fear the enemy any longer. You were baptized in the sea after you left Egypt. The enemy cannot feed on you any longer (just like salted meat or "biltong" cannot be spoiled). Your preservation in Christ means the enemies end (Gen 3:14). Your baptism is a prophetic proclamation of the enemy's end that will eventually be seen by all in future with our glorification, the new earth and Satan being cast in hell.

Only we could go through the water and only we could become part of the Eternal. The power of the enemy was only for a very limited period a problem in your life, but now it will never again be a problem, because we will never again lose our saltiness or the presence of Christ in us.

Day 11 What does the sea represent?

There is a shameless whore, a harlot or prostitute seated on many oceans or waters (Rev 17:1, CEV). The book of revelations is definitely not literal. Scripture always interprets Scripture. "The oceans, lakes, and rivers that the woman is sitting on represent masses of people of every race and nation (Rev 17:15, TLB)." People, races and nations are always illustrated as the sea, rivers, water or sand in the Bible. "But the wicked are like the restless sea - unable to be still, its waters toss up mud and dirt (Is 57:20, CJB)." Jude talk about ungodly people and say: "Raging waves of the sea, foaming out their own confusion; wandering stars, to whom the storm of darkness is reserved for ever (Jude 1:13, DRA)." There are many images of the tumultuous nations or the restless sea in the Bible (Jer 51:13, 42, 52). The moment you understand this image you will understand why 1. The lion with eagle wings (Nebuchadnezzar and the Babylonian empire), 2. The bear (the Medo-Persian Empire), 3. the Leopard with four wings and four heads (Alexander the Great and the 4 generals that succeeded him) and then the fourth beast with the ten horns (Roman empire) all came in succession in our history out of the "sea" (Dan 7:2, 3-7). The next Kingdom will be different. It will not come out of the sea, but from Heaven or out of the Cloud (Dan 7:13, 14). There were four world empires or kingdoms according to the Bible (the amount of man). The fourth still continuous to rule and regulate the earthly minded people through a worldly religious system, a social system, a political system and an economic system into which it was transformed (Dan 7:17, 19-21, 23-26). This unrighteous system is now running out of time and has very limited time left. "But the holy ones of the Most High God will receive that Kingdom which will last for all the ages to come, forever and ever (Dan 7:18, 22, 27, VOICE)."

I believe we are near to the generation that will see that happen!

Jacobus JJ Botha

Day 12 He will quiet the restless sea

Consider the Scriptures of yesterday. Can you see that the "sea" or rivers in the Bible resemble people in their turmoil and restlessness (Isaiah 57:20)? Assyria was the mighty water or river that broke its banks and that God used in the OT (Is 8:7). All the mighty waters throughout history was in His Hands and the waters of the future still is (Jer 47:1-4). "The Lord controls rulers, just as he determines the course of rivers (Prov 21:1, CEV).

Jesus prophesied that in our days the following would be signs to warn us of His coming: "The nations on earth will be afraid of the roaring sea and tides, and they won't know what to do (Luke 21:25, CEV)." We can see it clearly in the political, the social, the religious and the economic waves from all four corners of the earth (Rev 7:1-3). He reigns. He is completely in control. The turmoil of the people and nations will end when His Kingdom manifests. David prophesied it when he wrote: "He calmed the roar of seas, the roaring of the waves, and the turmoil of the peoples (Ps 65:7, ISV)." John saw the people of the Kingdom. They are calm, full of peace, without any pretentiousness and they are living before the throne of God (Rev 4:6). He is the One that will calm the nations. God will definitely bring His reign of peace over all the earth (Rev 15:2).

If you feel restless, come to Him. There is a calm river of Life and Inner Peace flowing from the throne of the Lamb (Rev 22:1). Come to Him irrespective of your original ocean or nation, race or tribe. He does not look or consider anything external. "The [Holy] Spirit and the bride (the church, believers) say, "Come." And let the one who hears say, "Come." And let the one who is thirsty come; let the one who wishes take and drink the water of life without cost (Rev 22:17, Amplified)."

Day 13 Rejoice! The end of the world system is near

The beast of Revelations 13:1-3 is arising from the nations or from the sea. The other and different kind of beast of Revelations is arising out of the earth (Rev 13:11). Please read Revelations 17:1 and 17:3 together. The harlot sits on many waters, but she is seen as sitting on the sand of the earth or in the desert (Rev 17:3). Can you see that "sea" = "sand" in the Bible. Do not build your house on the sand or do not be part of the restless sea.

The system that the enemy created rules over people from all the different kingdoms of this world (Rev 17:2). Satan is still deceiving the whole world through this harlot (Rev 12:9), except the chosen ones because it is not possible for him to do that (Matt 24:24). "Therefore rejoice, O heavens and you who dwell in them [in the presence of God] (Rev 12:12, Amplified)." Please see the two sides. We can rejoice! On the other hand God is warning both the earth and the sea (all nations from everywhere all over the earth). "Woe to the earth and the sea, because the devil has come down to you in great wrath, knowing that he has only a short time [remaining] (Rev 12:12, Amplified)!" God is not warning real fishes. No! We are the anglers who are catching and rescuing people from the restless sea or from the many different kinds of water of this world (all tribes, tongues, nations, races). We can rejoice, because we dwell in heaven forever! We are not part of the restless sea or the dust or the sand of this world anymore. This current world is not our home. We are spirit born from Spirit. We do not live according to the flesh anymore!

Day 14 The Sea was divided as a prophetic sign

"Adonai caused the sea to go back before a strong east wind all night. He made the sea become dry land, and its water was divided in two. Then the people of Isra'el went into the sea on the dry ground, with the water walled up for them on their right and on their left (Ex 14:21, 22, CJB)." With your baptism, God wants you to realize that He wants you to walk between two different kinds of people on this earth during your earthly journey (remember that Scripture showed us that the "sea" or many waters are "people" and nations). Your current walk was predestined for you for this time and age. Some people on your way will be the sheep on His Right Hand side. They will motivate and encourage you. The others will be the goats or the lovers of the world on His left that will distract you. There is a Wind that already started to blow since the darkest hour of the night or since the Great Tribulation. There is currently an even stronger Wind blowing from the East (Ex 14:21, 22). He is busy bringing division between water and water or water and sand or people and people (sheep and goats). The day is busy breaking. People will soon see what He did in His supremacy during the night! Let your baptism remind you not to focus on the sea or the people on your left hand side or the people on your right hand side, but to keep your focus on Almighty Adonai. He wants you to walk this earthly walk - that He predestined for you - with your focus and your trust constantly only on Him!

Day 15 Why did Jesus not swim in the water, but walked on it?

Some Christians are like the sea or like the people of the world. "The one who doubts is like a wave of the sea, blown and tossed around by the wind (James 1:6, NET)." Be different from the world. We do not have to be like the waves or restless sea of this world.

Jesus said: "Here on earth you will have many trials and sorrows. But take heart, because I have overcome the world (John 16:33, NLT)." Jesus walked on the water to demonstrate this truth and His victory over the world to us. He demonstrated to us that He walks in a higher dimension. He is higher than the "sea" or the restless people or nations of this world. It is only by being born again that we can share in His victory and join the higher dimension as Peter did. We can only walk on the water if we obey the Word. "For everyone born of God overcomes the world (1 John 5:4, NIV)." Peter could share this higher than the "sea" or "earth" dimension by Faith. When he started to focus on the world and lost his focus on the Word, he immediately became like them, sank under the grip of this present world and almost became part of the lower fleshly dimension or part of the sea, but Jesus rescued him.

Peter once sank into the water. Peter was once rescued from it. He experienced a baptism. Just like fallen man that once fell in sin and stayed under its influence, but was once rescued from it by the cross.

God is calling *you* out of the nations or out of the people to come and walk with Him in the higher dimension. It is a dimension of Grace, a dimension of unconditional Love, Mercy, kindness, forgiveness and servanthood and it is above earthly comprehension. Focus on Him. As long as you do, you will walk the walk of Faith or walk the impossible Heavenly walk.

Do not let the waters swallow you. God made us to walk on water!

Day 16 Baptized in the Cloud (Heaven) or Heavenly realm.

After the believers left Egypt, the enemy chased them and wanted to again submit them under the slavery of religion or dead works. There is a way (baptism) that God provided for His children. If the enemy or anything from the past tries to get hold of you and again try to bring you under subjection, cut off the grasp of the enemy on your life by going through the Red Sea.

The believers who left Egypt were not only baptized in the sea, but also in the Cloud. This is so precious. This is something that I cannot ever thank our heavenly Father adequately for. The moment the believers went through that water, they chose to be led by the Holy Spirit, by the Glorious Cloud, or by Heaven forever. They surrendered their rights of living their own independent lives or by following their own earthly ideas. They chose to become an intimate part of the Holy Spirit (or the only Spirit that is Holy in Himself) and of the spirit realm or Heaven forever. All the promises, Glory and covenants are in Heaven or in the Cloud preserved for us. Our protection, our provision and our guidance during day and during night are all in the Cloud. ("The God of the good times is also God of the bad times" and He will lead us through all circumstances. "The God of the day is also God of the night", the song says). See your enormous power and equipment in the Cloud. He leads you. You are part of the Cloud of Fire or the Cloud of Glory that will soon manifest His presence all over the earth, because you were baptized in the Cloud and became an integral part of Him forever. The Cloud will descend and purify the whole earth. God is before you like a Cloud, behind you like a Cloud and in you and above you (Is 52:12). We depend on His Right Hand and follow Him wherever He leads us. Cut of any illegal claim or grip that the enemy tries to get on you! Do it by the power of your baptism. See how that water brought division between you and the rulers of your past. See how it changed you from scarlet to snow in purity (part of the Cloud). See how it preserved you and how you were freed. The reign of the enemy and all his forces ended in your life.

Look forward! Look up. Embrace the Cloud. Move with the Cloud to the fullness of Christ. It must happen in the natural realm, even though you already have the fullness of Christ in you and in the Cloud ("For in Him we live and move and exist" (Acts 17:28, HCSB).

Day 17 Noah had to build the ark in order to survive the flood

"It was through faith that Noah, on receiving God's warning of impending disaster, reverently constructed an ark to save his household. This action of faith condemned the unbelief of the rest of the world, and won for Noah the righteousness before God *which follows such a faith* (Hebrews 11:7, Phillips)." Noah build an ark or an unsinkable temple consisting out of three divisions exactly like God told him (Gen 6:16). I want to warn every reader that the distress of this world can easily become bigger than you can budget and plan for in your own strength. "A rich person's wealth is his strong city and is like a high wall in his imagination. Before destruction a person's heart is arrogant (Prov 18:11, 12, NOG)." We must not become arrogant or fearful and cling to earthly securities shortly before the destruction or before the earthly systems will be destroyed. Earthly riches provide (and is) a false sense of security. It is a lie and that lie is active only in the minds or imaginations of those people being deceived by it. There is only One save Place. "The name of the Lord is a strong tower; the righteous runs to it and is safe and set on high [far above evil] (Prov 18:10, Amplified)."

Noah realized one thing in his inner being: "I must build an unsinkable and indestructible temple where God's family can be safe and stay protected. In the Name of Jesus, I call every man and every head of a family, to stand strong and help with the remaining bit of the building of God's house. We must be ready. A fixed decree regarding the total destruction of the current earthly systems was already signed with His blood in heaven on earth (Calvary – just like in the days of Noah). Build and work on your relationship with God. Build the congregation by loving her, serving her and speaking unashamed in their lives. Every minute that we continue to walk without the wall of water of the earthly system on our sides tumbling down on the worldly people to their own destruction, is only by Grace. We walk by Grace every step. Grace, just Grace! He gives us time to help more people to cross the Red Sea. We can rescue more people from the false securities of Pharaoh. Come on men. Let us give our lives for this building as

Noah did (Hag 2:4). Our time is limited on this present earth and our task is big!

Day 18 Baptized in Christ!

We already saw that we were once baptized 1. In the sea (in order to remind us that we are the salt of the earth). It also reminds us of our walk that God predestined for us between the different kinds of people around us specifically at this time and age (Acts 17:26). We are also baptized 2. in the Cloud (as shadow type of the Spirit of Go

d) that guides us day and night and in whom we live, move and have our being (Acts 17:27, 28).

God is Spirit, but He took on the form of flesh and blood in order to reveal Himself to us in the physical realm in order for us to see and know who and how He is in Spirit (as Spirit cannot be seen).

The people in the OT were also baptized in Moses under whose guidance they walked (1 Cor 10:2). Moses was temporary and he died! We do not follow him (the law) like they did. Grace leads us. We are followers of Christ. We follow the Christ in us. Like the sea and like the cloud, Moses was also just a shadow of 3. The Fullness that came in Christ (and in whose Kingdom we now stand and live in spirit in the New Testament). During the baptism in the Old Testament (Red Sea), the people submitted and associated themselves with the fullness of their souls to the guidance of Moses their leader in the seen realm. We also associated ourselves with Christ in our baptism. We submitted ourselves to Christ's Government in the spirit realm or to His guidance or the Kingdom in the Cloud that can only be experienced through His clouds (us). We are baptized in Christ Jesus our Lord. We are intimately associated with Him. He is the chosen Lamb of God or the elected Life, the Power, the Love and the Grace of our Father that will manifest through us and the One that will be seen through us with our glorification.

Christ is our new identity. Baptism is there to help you fix your identity in Him alone (and in nothing of this world). We are Christ(ians) to the world. Only He as Person can guide us to the fullness of who we are in Spirit. Christ is the Only Way. He came when we were lost and when we could not see any possible way of ever touching God and ever being reconciled with Him. You are an irrevocable part of the Living Word. Your complete and absolute identification with Him by being baptized in Him, reminds you of this eternal Truth. You are in Him and He is the living Word in you. You are a living Bible to others. They see Him in you!

Day 19 Baptized into one body

Since man fell into sin, death or separation rules on earth. Our bodies and souls are still not in harmony with our spirits or with what happened and was done for us during the resurrection of Christ after that cross (the cross that He carried on our behalves by His Grace). We are still scattered like the dead bones in the valley in our pride and in our rebellion against Truth (Ezek 37). The reason why the enemy will try everything in his power to keep us separated is that he knows that our unity is our strength. The longer he can keep us in defending our own religious doctrines and not submit to Scripture, the longer we will fight each other and not be able to make any real difference in the world. God is busy restoring unity. The different parts of the body will first come together or unity will first be restored, and then God is going to empower us as the mightiest army the universe has ever seen (Ezek 37:7-11). It is not only we as Christians that believe that God is One. No, the devils or fallen angels know it. The absolute Oneness or absolute and complete undivided unity between Father, Son and Holy Spirit is of such a nature that they tremble (James 2:19)! God has the same unity or oneness in mind for His church. Your baptism will remind you of this: "For by one Spirit we are all baptized into one body, whether we are Jews or Gentiles, whether we are slaves or free, and we have all been made to drink of one Spirit (1 Cor 12:13, MEV)."

Day 20 Our unification will open up new heavenly dimensions to walk in!

The people on earth decided to all stand together in unity with the enemy in religion at Babel. The enemy always want you to anchor yourself or your mind and settle at a place of religion where you will no longer be able to move with the Cloud or with the Holy Spirit to the Fullness or Glorification of Christ. The enemy absolutely likes it when people say: "This is my church doctrine. I will die for it. I will not be moved. We will gather around this doctrine or theology and build our kingdom, instead of helping people to gather around Christ as Person."

"And the Lord said, Behold, they are one people and they have all one language; and this is only the beginning of what they will do, and *now nothing they have imagined they can do will be impossible for them* (Gen 11:6, AMPC)."

Can you see the power in unity? "Come on! Let's go down and confuse them by making them speak different languages—then they won't be able to understand each other (Gen 11:7, CEV)." We will never find our unity in religion anymore. God allows and is causing all the confusion in religious circles (in Babel or at Babylon) simply because He wants His children to be united in Him only and not in any external denominational doctrines. He wants you to have an intimate walk with Him. He does not want you to join any of the millions of different camps of religious divisions. There is only unity in Christ! When He is lifted up, all men will be drawn to Him (John 12:32).

"For even as the body is one and yet has many members, and all the members of the body, though they are many, are one body, so also is Christ (1 Cor 12:12, NASB)." This translation is correct. Christ is a many membered body. This statement speaks about the Reality of His being. It is not a comparison.

"For by one Spirit we were all baptized into one body, whether Jews or Greeks, whether slaves or free, and we were all made to drink of one Spirit (1 Cor 12:13, NASB)." We lost our own individual lives at the cross. The baptism is to remind you that you are part of a single body consisting of different members. We are all uniquely different, but we are all part of who Christ is. This is why there is no competition between us, but only completion. We do not live for ourselves, for our previous identities on this earth or for our own needs anymore. No, we live to encourage and build others or the body so that they can excel. Your baptism reminds you that we all need each other.

As soon as there will be manifested unity in the body of Christ, absolutely nothing in heaven or earth will be impossible for the church! The enemy knows it. He and his forces tremble! The unified church will rule and reign the new earth forever!

Day 21 Let only the Word speak through Scripture

"Make every effort to keep the oneness of the Spirit in the bond of peace [each individual working together to make the whole successful]. There is one body [of believers] and one Spirit—just as you were called to one hope when called [to salvation] - one Lord, one faith, one baptism, one God and Father of us all who is [sovereign] overall and [working] through all and [living] in all (Eph 4:3-6, Amplified)." "By one Spirit we were all baptized into one body (1 Cor 12:13, GWT)." "All of you together are Christ's body, and each of you is a part of it (1 Cor 12:27, NLT)." "Is not the bread which we break a sharing in the body of Christ? Since there is one bread, we who are many are one body; for we all partake of the one bread (1 Cor 10:16, 17, NASB). "Have we not all one Father? Has not one God created us? Why then do we deal faithlessly and treacherously each against his brother, profaning the covenant of [God with] our fathers? (Malachi 2:10, AMPC)." "For just as each of us has one body with many members, and these members do not all have the same function, so in Christ we, though many, form one body, and each member belongs to all the others (Romans 12:4, 5, NIV)." "If you have two shirts, give one to the poor. If you have food, share it with those who are hungry (Luke 3:11, NLT)." "All the believers were united in heart and mind. And they felt that what they owned was not their own, so they shared everything they had (Acts 4:32, NLT)."

We know so much and have so much knowledge of Scripture, but the day will come and it is almost here, where we will also walk in this knowledge.

Day 22 Bad fruit when ignoring the message of the baptism

I want to say so much based on the verses I quoted yesterday, but I sit with tears in my eyes over so many broken people and countries in the world. I know so many people that feel they want to and need to flee from other people.

Whenever there is division, there is death. "Division" = "death". Divided countries experience so much death and turmoil! The same for divided families. The ignorant CEO's are mainly responsible and not firstly the followers. We are all sometimes astonished at how people can experience increasing pain without repentance or without willing to change their ways (Rev 9:20, 21, 16:9, 11)! We see and know that God has a great future in mind for us if we will only humble ourselves and realize that we are one in Truth, one in Grace, one in Love or one in Him! "Behold, how good and how pleasant it is for brothers to dwell together in unity! For there the Lord has commanded the blessing: life forevermore (Ps 133:1, 3, Amplified)." I pray that God will bring His Peace and healing in your life first. May He calm the storm in your life. May He free us from any turmoil or frustration, fear, rejection or whatever the symptoms that you or I might experience due to division. May He bring healing where there is a lack of harmony or a lack of "Rest" or still "division" in yourself. I also pray this for your family and for your larger community. May God bring rest and may His Peace be with you always!

"The God of peace will soon crush Satan under your feet" (Rom 16:20, ESV). Soon the victory and glory of the resurrected Christ will manifest through His body.

Day 23 Night is the time to be on guard, to watch and to be ready (Mark 13:36-37).

We know that darkness covered the earth after Jesus left the seen realm. Due to the Great Tribulation and dark Middle ages (night) the church lost all light or revelation of Christ. She walked in almost complete darkness and became extremely weak. Her light was almost non-existent. She was the smoldering wick that Matthew talked about in the Bible, but now His justice will grant her the promised victory (Matt 12:20, CEB).

Night was a reality to all of us, whether it was individual man or corporate man trying to do a "separated-from-Him" thing.

It is important for a "watchman" or guard to be able to estimate how much of the night is left. Jesus said: "Therefore, be continually on the alert—for you do not know when the master of the house is coming, whether 1. In the evening, or 2. At midnight, or 3. When the rooster crows, or 4. In the morning (Mark 13:35, Amplified with own numbering added)." In the Bible or in history the night was divided in four portions. *All four* portions of night (the dark reign of man) was there for man to try and prove that he can do his own thing, but he had to learn and discover that all his own effort and struggles were to no avail. Both "4" and "6" are the numbers of man. So keep the four portions of man in mind, as it is prophetic.

From 18:00 to 21:00 was evening in Biblical nights, from 21:00 to 24:00 was midnight, from 00:00 to 03:00 was the "crowing of the rooster"-time and from 03:00 to 06:00 was early in the morning or dawn. Soldiers that stood guard understood and made use of these shifts.

The Israelites took the biggest part of the night to cross the Red Sea during their baptism. During the morning watch (the last part of the night or the early dawn), everything came to a climax (Ex 14:24). God intervened miraculously from the Cloud. The Egyptians were destroyed during the last watch or during the last shift of the night (Ex 14:27).

God's timing during "their baptism" was prophetic regarding our time. People are starting to fear, because the enemy became so arrogant. At this very moment, the children of the world are busy intimidating God's children in their Egyptian or worldly arrogance (like Noah experienced and prophesied for our time). Do not fear! The way you see the enemy now, will soon end. People will stop relying on their own plans, submit to Christ, trust in Him, and call on Him (Ex 14:13, 14). The day starts to break. The church is busy arising all over the globe. The enemy has limited time! Our God is not asleep. He will intervene miraculously during the final climax.

Day 24 He will test your trust to the ultimate limits

Yesterday we saw how God miraculously intervened during the baptism in the Red Sea. He left the Israelites the whole night in their panic while He watched them from His presence with them in the Cloud. Heaven guarded them through that Cloud of fire that the enemy could not access, but God only finally intervened during the break of the new day.

This historic event reminded me of how Christ allowed Jacob to struggle the whole night with Him at Peniel. God only gave him his breakthrough when the day was breaking (Gen 32:24). Jesus compelled or constrained His disciples to cross the sea even though He knew a storm was coming (Mark 6:45, Matt 14:22). He went to the mountain to pray (Mark 6:46, Matt 14:23). The fact that He "left" them and went up the mountain was prophetic regarding His ascension into heaven and leaving them "on their own". He probably prayed the same prayer for them that He prayed for Peter (Luke 22:32). He saw that the wind was against them and that they struggled, but He did not intervene during their test (Mark 6:48). They were in the middle of the lake when night fell (Mark 6:47). They were still not on the other side during the last portion or the fourth watch of the night. They struggled for at least 9 hours plus. They must have been very exhausted and with no strength of their own left. It is prophetic of our struggle with the world. He came miraculously. The sea was the disciples' normal work environment that got out of hand for them. They could not handle it out of their own efforts any longer. We all struggle in this world (the "sea"). Like them, we are all in the same boat. They did not expect God to come in the way He did. They thought it was a ghost and screamed out of fear. He calmed them by saying: "Take heart! *I Am!* Stop being alarmed and afraid (Mark 6:50, AMPC)." He got in the boat and the storm stopped.

Day 25 After He joined them, the harvest followed!

The new day was about to break at the time that Jesus finally joined His disciples when He returned from the mountain (Heaven). They struggled the whole night "without Him". He changed everything with His manifested presence (prophetic regarding His second appearance or His second coming). "Then those in the boat worshiped Him [with awe-inspired reverence], saying, 'Truly You are the Son of God!' (Matt 14:33, Amplified)."

The disciples in the boat are prophetic and represents us as the adult children of God. It will again happen like this for us at the time and moment of His second appearance (or when He will "come back").

"They had not understood [the miracle of] the loaves [how it revealed the power and deity of Jesus]; but [in fact] their heart was hardened [being oblivious and indifferent to His amazing works] (Mark 6:52, Amplified)." (Exactly like the hardened hearts of the people in the world now while "He is gone" to the "top of the mountain" or Heaven to intercede for us – Heb. 7:25, Rom 8:34).

Can you now see why He had to let them (and us) struggle so that they (we) could come to the end of themselves (ourselves)? Together they experienced the new day (of Christ). It will be a marvelous day of reconciliation for us! The day of Christ is almost breaking. It is already the last part or the fourth watch of the night. Do not think that He did not watch us and did not test our trust in Him during the night. Our test will soon be over. He likes to test our Love for Him and our Trust in Him, but He will never test us beyond what we can bear (1 Cor 10:13). He is on His way. His reward of Eternal Glory for you as His faithful servant is with Him. His manifest and seen presence will soon change everything. The enemy gave us a hard time during the night (all the time that man tried to do it in their own effort), but the enemy's time is over. The Prince of Peace will soon be here!

One whole and long night they all struggled with the world. They struggled and tried to stay on top of the "sea" or the people or earthly nations and worldly systems that tried to swallow them in. The sea made it extremely difficult for them (us). After He joined them, all the people came out of their towns, the cities and the surrounding areas to Him and all were healed (Mark 6:56). It is all prophetic regarding His second coming. These miracles and events mentioned in the Bible that those people experienced, are all waiting for the day of Christ that is now busy breaking. We will soon heal and harvest the nations for His Kingdom in the day of Christ that is definitely coming! The sea will be calmed (worldly systems in their restlessness will disappear). Only the King will receive all glory and honor from all of us as His fishers of people. Even the Thomas's will see and believe! What a glorious day it will be.

Day 26 Baptism is still a declaration in public or a sign of our repentance from sin!

John the Baptist was the first person to baptize people. He got the command from God. His baptism was before the cross. It was a baptism of repentance or death only and it still is one part or one leg of our baptism in Christ. What is repentance? It is to reckon yourself dead to sin (Rom 6:11).

What is sin? Jesus beautifully explained it when He mentioned three things that He wants us to know (during our baptism) that will make us strong in our minds or souls and help us to walk victoriously in this current earth. He said about the Holy Spirit: "And He, when He comes, will convict the world about 1. [The guilt of] sin [and the need for a Savior], 2. And about righteousness, 3. And about judgment (John 16:8, Amplified but with my own numbering). Then Jesus started to explain the statement that He just made. He said: "About sin, because they do not believe in Me [trust in, rely on, and adhere to Me] (John 16:9, AMPC)". Can you see from this definition that Jesus gave is that "sin" is unbelief in Christ? Wrong deeds only result from unbelief or separation from Christ and is only symptoms of unbelief. Sin is "unbelieve" or the act where a person does not want to believe due to pride, independence or self-sufficiency! Your baptism is therefore the sacrament, sign or confession in public that you turned your back on your previous life that you lived in unbelief (The previous life of independence and before you were born again or convicted of your need for a Savior). You now reckon yourself dead with your baptism for the life of an unbeliever and all the symptoms that spread out of such a life separated from Christ.

Day 27 I woke up with a "thanks-for-you" in my heart on this lovely day

"Then Jesus' mother and brothers came to see him, but they couldn't get to him because of the crowd. Someone told Jesus, "Your mother and your brothers are outside, and they want to see you." Jesus replied, 'My mother and my brothers are all those who hear God's word and obey it' (Luke 8:19-21, 1953)." Jesus lifted out a truth that most carnal Christians (lukewarm) or fleshly people cannot understand. Jesus never rejected the people of His fleshly family or those connected to Him through an earthly birth or connection. He loved them, but His real compassion and biggest love was for His spirit family or those born out of Him and also driven by Him. His heart and passion was one with those in front of Him that were near to Him and those that also experienced the drive and burning zeal of the Living Word or Spirit. I personally love people in general. There are many people that I know and love and it includes my family on both sides and near friends, but there are certain people with whom I feel one in Spirit. We can talk about Jesus and His coming Kingdom as far as their appetites allow them. These are the very dearest and most special people in my life, because I can just relax and open my mouth to allow the fullness in my heart to overflow. My very close friends and family know that I often feel like Jeremiah in Jeremiah 20:9. Many people crossed our way so far, but not every person are with you on the Road to Emmaus (Luke 24:32). There are very special people so near and so dear to us, and I have never told them just how precious they are. Thanks for every person who reads this. It speaks. Especially thanks to that core group who walked with us for so long! My heart and my being are with you and you are constantly in our prayers. Thanks for all feedback. Thanks also to the people who do not want me to talk about baptism, the gifts of the Holy Spirit, the fact that we died for the law written on dead stone tablets etc. May God bring us all to the adulthood that He predestined for us as His church! May you all be ready for His appearance to and through us (or the glorification of our bodies)! May you share in the joy of harvesting the whole world and the nations for His Kingdom that will soon come! Your heart will thrill and tremble with the joy of seeing the harvest coming to Him! We were made for being fishers of men! Nothing else on earth will ever excite you nearly as much! Nothing else is even worth mentioning or comparing to this noble call! I honestly love you in Christ! Thanks!!!

Day 28 He is the "α" (Bethlehem) to "Ω" (ascension)

The word alphabet is derived from a combination of the first two letters of the Greek alphabet. The first letter is alpha or "α" and it looks like a fish swimming from East to West. (*Please read Ps. 103:12 and Matt. 24:27 - Selah*). Christ is the "Alpha" or First Light (and only Light) from the [Middle] East that came to this "sea" (or this dark world full of "fishes") in order to bring His enlightenment or Glory to all of us. He is the Big and Strong Alpha "A", but became weak and as a baby or "α". There will be no end to the increase of His Government.

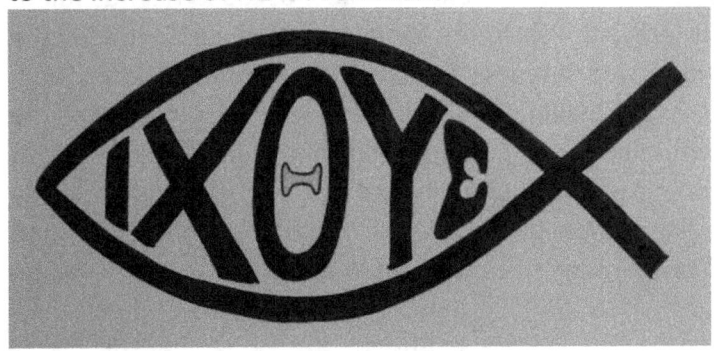

ι	Jesus
χ	Christ
θ	of God
γ	Son
∑	Savior

Please keep in mind that Christ is the Capital Omega "Ω". He came to make us fishers of men. Through us He wants to complete the task of saving the whole world that He had (has) in mind. Nothing less.

Throughout the ages, Christians always identified themselves with the Alpha. He is our Origin. He is our Beginning "α" or "A" and He is our "ω" Omega "Ω" or the Big One (Fish) that moved upward or the ascending One. He is our All and Everything possible from "α" or "A" to "ω" or "Ω". There is nothing that you can imagine (or spell) that does not exist because of Him and for His Ultimate glory in the end. "For from Him and through Him and to Him are all things. [For all things originate with Him and come from Him; all things live through Him, and all things center in and tend to consummate and to end in Him.] To Him be glory forever! Amen (Rom 11:36, AMPC)."

He came as a small child "α" from the East, but He turned His face to heaven and "swam" upwards as an adult "Ω" and finally left like this during His ascension.

Christians throughout the ages associated themselves with Him and from there the symbol of the "Fish". The word "ixtus" that we see inside the fish in ancient excavations (and still on Christian cars, houses and key holders), is formed from five Greek letters. Five is the amount of Grace, because He was full of Grace and Mercy. Greek is the language of the NT. It was the *world language* associated with wisdom. He is our Wisdom. The 5 letters or Message inside the Fish invites people from all over the world (the whole sea) to come to Him and follow the "Ω". This invitation is not just for one family and just all that family's fleshly children or one nation only. No! The blood of Jacob cannot and will never compare to the blood of the Lamb. Do not ever be deceived!

("i" = Jesus, "x" = Christ, "tu" = God's Son, 's' = Saviour). Just worship and honor God for His wisdom. Do not stay in "the sea". Turn you face to heaven and swim upward the way He did as the "Ω". Read Matthew 5:8, but beware of the people who see ghosts, demons and wrongs in all things and miss Him! Remember that all is holy for them that are holy (Titus 1:15). (Refuse to let the enemy blind you to see His glory and rob you from your worship. Give the devil no honor for an association that so many Christians died for! You may wear a cross and you may cherish this symbol as well). Absolutely nothing wrong with it.

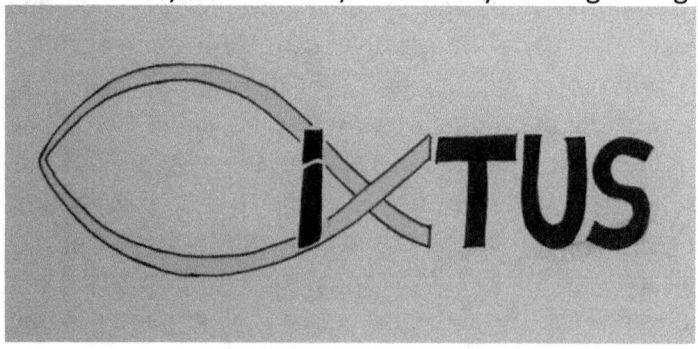

Day 29 Eat Him! His body was broken for us!

He is not only the "Bread" or "Manna" from Heaven. No, the "Fish" (OT and NT) that was broken also represent His body. His body was broken for us to eat so that we can be satisfied and live forever (Matt 14:17-19, Luke 9:16, Mark 6:41). He broke Himself by a voluntary act on that cross. He broke the bread and fish and gave it to us, we must just hand the Food out of His Hand to the hungry and the needy. Eating Him or eating the Word has nothing to do with cannibalism. No! Do not think as the carnal minded or the worldly people with their shallow fleshly minds. No! To eat the Word is more than just reading Scripture or just listening to a sermon. It is to pray about it and meditate it day and night (Deut 11:18-20, Rom 10:8). It is like chewing your food, digesting it mechanically and then chemically so that it can finally be absorbed by your body and become part of you or one with you. The food must strengthen your body, nourish it and mean something to it. The same is true for the Word. We must not only read Scripture, but also associate ourselves 100 % with the Word and do what He says. He must build you. He must be your strength and your all. When Jesus told His disciples that He is not interested in them just being saved, but they must eat His flesh and drink His blood, most left Him. This was too much asked! That command will cost you. They wanted miracles, blessings, prosperity, money and all that Egypt can offer them in order to try and satisfy their earthly lusts with, but to walk in covenant with a Person whose Kingdom , Glory, absolute intimacy and unity (to be one with Him) you constantly desire, was/is too much asked for them.

I am here to invite you to the feast of the Alpha that we must follow. He is the Alpha or your very beginning. You were created out of Him and to follow Him. He is the broken "Fish" from Heaven whose body was broken for you. Come and eat with us from the Manna and/or the Broken Bread from Heaven and be strengthened in your spirits. He liked "fish" and intimately became part of us! He also lived for us!

"Come", I command you in His Name: "Come", hear His invitation. Many were invited (Luke 14:15-21), but most had "valid" earthly excuses. "Come", there is space and still time to join the feast of broken Bread and broken Fish in the Kingdom (Luke 14:23-35)!

If you have any excuse and He is not really your Alpha, you will not taste Him and will not share His Glory (Luke 14:24). "You treat me to a feast, while my enemies watch. You honor me as your guest, and you fill my cup until it overflows Ps 23:5, CEV)." May the nations hear and see your overflow!

Day 30 See their real need and satisfy their real hunger!

"You have made people like the fish in the sea, like the sea creatures that have no ruler (Hab 1:14, NIV)."

We need a ruler. We are like fish or as stupid as sheep on our own. We need God's guidance. "However, in order not to give offense and cause them to stumble [that is, to cause them to judge unfavorably and unjustly] go down to the sea and throw in a hook. Take the first fish that comes up, and when you open its mouth you will find there a shekel. Take it and give it to them to pay the temple tax for Me and for yourself (Matt 17:27, AMPC)."

God wants us to know that the Person that He elected to be First is Superior to all of us. All miracle working Life or Supernatural Life is only in Him. Carefully look at His Mouth. In His Mouth or in His Word is all the provision that we will ever need while on this corruptible earth. He will provide in order for us to satisfy the requirements (like taxations) from this earthly systems. He is the Alpha that will provide miraculously in your needs and even to the smallest detail. Just do what He tells you to do. You will be surprised at His foreknowledge and attention to detail.

He is the One that we must tell our kids about so that they can enter the City of David or the New Jerusalem either through the Sheepgate (Pastoral ministry) or the **Fish**gate (Evangelical ministry) (Nehemiah 3:1, 3). Do not be a bad parent. Your child needs Jesus. You need to evangelize and feed him or her. Our children have a hunger for the Bread of Life; do not just give them more laws on morality. They need Bread, not an indigestible stone (or stone tablet). They need a Person! (Matt 7:9). This is why Jesus said: "Would you give your child a snake if the child asked for a Fish (Matt 7:10, CEV)." Why will you give them the world and all the earthly riches or things of the snake (Satan) when their real need is the Alpha and Omega (or Fish or Bread of heaven)? You can spoil your child in life and give him or her whatever their hearts desire, but if you failed to tell them about Jesus, you have given them the snake and not the Person they really needed and asked for! Do not think Jesus just say things without a deeper meaning. Cherish His Word! The Word is Spirit and Life!

Day 31 It was to make Him known to the people of Israel that I came and baptized

We all sinned. God is not just overlooking sin. No! He cannot just sweep it under the carpet as if it never happened or just ignore it. He strictly condemned it! Somebody had to pay for it. If God just accepted it or just forgave it without Somebody paying for it, He would have collaborated with evil or giving His approval to it. No, He is holy. He cannot stand sin or cannot tolerate it. That is why sinners are condemned to an eternal existence separated from His presence (hell). Unfortunately, all people on earth were contaminated with sin. All people lived in separation from God and separated from the spirit realm. We needed Somebody in the Spirit realm to pull us back into the higher spiritual dimension from where we fell when man sinned in the garden (just like people who were busy drowning in a pit of mud had to be rescued by somebody on the outside standing on dry and solid Rock and able to pull them out).

It was clearly prophesied that God would come as our Savior and that He would die for the sins of the whole world (Is 53, Ps 22:16-18, 34:20, 109:4, Zech 12:10 etc.). Jesus came. He walked in Heaven while on earth (John 3:13). He came to pay and to rescue us out of this pool of mud or out of this evil and miry world of dust. Jesus knew He came to save us and therefore He went to John to be baptized (Matt 16:21). John recognized Him while he was busy baptizing the people in the Jordan with the confession of their sins. He shouted: "Behold, the Lamb of God, who takes away the sin of the world (John 1:29, ESV)!" They had to behold the Lamb, because their baptism and our baptism would not mean anything without beholding the Lamb. It will be a total empty ritual.

"This is the Man I meant when I said, 'A Man comes after me who is always in front of me, for He existed before I was born!' It is true I have not known Him, yet it was to make Him known to the people of Israel that I came and baptized people with water (John 1:30, 31, Philips)."

I pray that the meaning of your baptism will reveal Him in a bigger measure to you.

Day 32 The Spirit raised Him from the water grave

Jesus was/is the Lamb of God from Heaven (from Eternity or from the Eternal Realm or from the Spirit realm). NB: The Lamb went willingly to John that was out of the tribe of Levi (or the priests called by God) in the Jordan to be baptized (John 1:29, 10:18). John then saw the perfect and sinless Lamb of God and proclaimed His beauty and His superior Being (Matt 3:14). He laid his hands upon Jesus's head and the sin of the world was placed prophetically on Jesus Christ our Lord (Lev 4:29, 33 etc.). Jesus was now prophetically contaminated with all the sins of the whole world through all ages and both symbolically and prophetically, He had to die. John (the priest called and named by God) therefore immersed Him or baptized Him in the water. Jesus went down in the water grave just as He would later die, be placed into the grave, enter the heart of the earth, and be separated from His earthly Life or Body. His baptism by man emphasized that His death and the way He would enter the grave would also be by the hands of man.

Jesus did not stay under the water or in that water grave. A miraculous event took place after John placed Jesus's body under the water. Heaven suddenly opened (Luke 3:21 - Selah). The Holy Spirit came visibly like a dove down from Heaven and raised Jesus prophetically from that grave of water while Jesus was praying. The Voice spoke loud and clear from Heaven: "You are My beloved Son; in You I am well pleased (Luke 3:22, BSB)."

John baptized in order for Jesus to be revealed. Here the revelation of the biggest mystery in the Universe played off in front of the eyes of the whole world to see and for them to know who He was and what His intended mission and purpose was. Can you see that the baptism of Jesus was prophetic? Jesus knew in His mind that His Spirit would again come and be reconciled with His Body and raise Him from the real grave and from the death that He would sink into due to His cross (just as His Spirit prophetically rose Him from that water grave at that moment of His baptism). His prophetic death and resurrection was such a reality in His mind during His baptism, that He walked by Faith in the power of the resurrection from that very moment of His baptism. In His mind, it was as good as if He already died and as if He was already raised from the death after paying for our sin or unbelief and all the terror that spread from that. Jesus knew His Father would later at Calvary declare Him (and all of humanity) Righteous with the power of a physical resurrection from the death and thereby declare Him with Heavenly Power and Authority as His beloved Son or the Anointed One in whom He is well-pleased (Rom 4:25). It is only because it was a 100 % certainty in His mind that the Voice from Heaven spoke and could be heard (**Selah**). This was the very moment that heaven opened for Jesus (Matt 3:16). It was the very moment that He was declared as an adult Son of God (Matt 3:17). From this moment on, He could clearly see in Heaven, hear every command from the Spirit or from our Spirit Father with 100 % accuracy. His walk on earth was 100 % different after His baptism compared to the way it was before it. His walk in the open heaven on earth was one of Power, Might, Glory and Authority. This was the Mirror image or revelation of how the sons of God (adult children) will also soon walk on this earth. (Please read this message repeatedly and please meditate and pray on this until it is revealed to you)

Day 33 As a young believer, I was so arrogant!

"He must not be a recent convert, so that he won't become arrogant, ISV)." "He must not be a new Christian, or he might become arrogant (1 Tim 3:6, GWT)." This portion of Scripture describes me, in 1994 to 1997. I was there. God gave me the revelation of the baptism in 1994. I wanted to go and discuss it at the synod and with the highest level of our denominational leaders when they gathered, but they did not allow me to. In spite of my earnest begging and pleas in that regard and for them to hear what I have to say and compare it to Scripture, they expelled us and completely rejected us. We just wanted to discuss the Truth that God revealed to us in love, but they closed their ears. I then wrote a book to explain what God showed me in order to be heard, but again withdrew it from the market in 1998 and shortly after being published. I was in reaction against the systems that were keeping people from seeing the Truth. I wanted the whole world to know and see the Truth, but I deeply sinned with the things I did in own strength (1 Tim 3:6). We still carry the scars of deep wounds that we obtained in this battle for Truth! God showed me my character of arrogance and hardness. He convinced us to speak the Truth in Love irrespective of the opinion of people (but to be gentle, not hard and to only share it with people that want to know (1 Pet. 3:15). We still daily pray for His Grace and Love to guide us. God forgave me for trying to persuade people in my own strength in the past. I learned and saw through the years that people without a hunger to know Him mostly reject the Truth. I want to proclaim Him, because everybody will ultimately recognize Him as the Chief Corner Stone. People will eventually choose Him and Scripture above denominational doctrines. In the end, all knees will bow before Him. He will be esteemed higher than any dead denominational doctrines or any idolatry that so many of us as religious people are currently involved in.

Day 34 The cross stands at the center of the universe

God said in Scripture that the earthly Jerusalem is the center of the earth and of all the nations according to the way He sees it (Ezek 5:5, 38:12). That is the reason why He chose this city and this specific place in the OT to display His Glory. The very center point of the universe is found in the exact spot where the cross of Calvary was planted. The whole universe emanated from the exact spot and place where the Lamb was crucified back in Eternity and long before the foundation of the earth (Rev 13:8). All nations around Jerusalem had to see the cross. They had to hear the message of His death for our sin in the market place. The cross will always be the center of the gospel. This is why the message of Romans 6 forms the center of what God believes. We as Christians can share in God's Faith, as we do not have any Faith out of ourselves – Gal 2:20, 3:22, Rom 3:22. Paul said in Romans 6:1 that we will not continue to sin, because we died for it. How? The whole of humanity was represented on those three crosses on Calvary. All of us have very limited time before it is time to exhale our last breath as sinners, just as those sinners had limited time while hanging on those crosses. We deserve death just like they did, because all of us sinned at a certain time in our lives and fell short from the Glory that God predestined for us (Rom 3:23). Christians and non-Christians all die in the same manner in the eyes of the world, but it is the state of spiritual maturity that we die in that will make the eternal difference (Rom 14:8). Our physical deaths or earthly departures will also be seen and witnessed by the people around us just like it was with those people dying on those crosses in the presence of the Lamb (Is 53:12). Some people will choose Christ and choose to be with Him in His kingdom and they will be his witnesses to the crowds. Others will reject Him until their final breath. This will happen because the cross is the place where He already separated the sheep or the people on His right hand side from the goats on His left hand side. Some will recognize the Man in the middle for who He is. They will honour Him in front of all for who He is. Others will reject Him in front of all with their short earthly lives, words and deeds. They will die and enter eternal death or eternal separation from Him. He is so fair. We all have a choice, but we all have such limited time!

Day 35 We died and rose with Him. We share His Holy Heavenly Life!

It was prophesied: "He will again have compassion on us; He will vanquish our iniquities. You will cast all our sins into the depths of the sea (Micah 7:19, HCSB)." "I, even I, am He Who blots out and cancels your transgressions, for My own sake, and I will not remember your sins (Is 43:25, AMPC)."

Christ died after He took our sins on Him in Gethsemane. He rose again because our sins were left in hell or separated from Him and separated from His Royal family members (you) forever. "He has removed our sins from us as far as the east is from the west (Ps 103:12)! Our sins were left in that place of separation that is separated from Him and separated from His Eternal glory (that place is called hell) and it cannot ever be found again or even be called in remembrance (Heb 8:12). God's mind and thoughts are so filled with the delight of your complete and perfect redemption that He will not sit and think about your sins and meditate on accusations against you. No! He is for us and not against us like the accuser is. His ears are not open to gossip about you or suspicion concerning your relationship with Him. God and the enemy has two complete different thought patterns and those thoughts originate out of two complete opposite realms.

"Or aren't you aware that all of us who were baptized into Christ Jesus were baptized into His death? We therefore were buried with Him through baptism into death, in order that, just as Christ was raised from the dead through the glory of the Father, we too may walk in newness of life. For if we have been united with Him like this in His death, we will certainly also be raised to life as He was (Rom 6:3-5, BSB)."

The glory that you must see during your baptism in Christ is that just as He died to sin, we also died for it. That is why you now have victory over it. Just as He was raised from the death, we were also raised from that separation from God (or death) and we can now intimately walk with Him in the newness of life here and now on this earth! Enjoy your victory in Him and your fellowship with Him!

Day 36 Revision

"He shall lay his hand on the head of the sin offering and slay the sin offering at the place of the burnt offering (Lev 4:29, NASB)." Sin in the OT was placed on a perfect lamb by the laying on of hands. After that was done, the Lamb was killed in order to get rid of that sin and in order to separate it from the land of the living. Jesus was the Perfect Lamb of God. Jesus's baptism was prophetic. It pointed forward to His death at Calvary that would follow. The moment John placed the sin of the world on the Lamb of God that had to be slain (Lev 4:29, 33 etc.), Jesus died prophetically. Why? Because the enemy could get a hold or grip on Him because of the sin. Sin will rob you from your spiritual strength, power and your authority in the Name of Jesus Christ. The enemy knows it and immediately attacked even Jesus in His physical weakness after His fast. The enemy lost his grip on Jesus in His death, because our Lamb was sinless. He rose from that water grave and walked in the Power of an open Heaven after He prophetically died for our sins during His water baptism, but there was another baptism that Jesus had in mind for all of us to see. Jesus said to them. "Can you drink the cup I have to drink? Can you go through the baptism I have to bear (Mark 10:38, Phillips)?" "...we suffer with Him, so that we may also be glorified together "(Rom. 8:17, BLB). When Jesus later took the sin of the world upon Himself by drinking the cup in Gethsemane, the enemy came, arrested Him and killed Him in His weakness. He died or lost His earthly Life on our behalf. Again, the Holy Spirit came and raised Him from His physical death on that cross of Calvary (exactly as it happened during His prophetical death and resurrection during His baptism). A 100 % replica of His water baptism, but this time the cruel and glorious reality that could be seen in His real death on Calvary and His resurrection in this physical realm.

Day 37 Your own baptism is also prophetic

God said: "When you go through deep waters, I will be with you. When you go through rivers of difficulty, you will not drown. When you walk through the fire of oppression, you will not be burned up; the flames will not consume you (Is 43:2, NLT)." God will always raise you up on the other side (Rom 8:37)! Even if the waters are as deep as death itself, you will be victorious in His Name. Please do not quit! We saw how Israel miraculously went through the water, but the Egyptians or non-believers were not raised on the other side because they did not have Faith to pass through the water.

Your own water baptism was also prophetic of your own physical death that will one day follow. We all face the shadow of death. You can rest in your last moments while facing your physical departure from the physical realm (physical death or separation from your loved ones on earth). You can know that: just as you came out on the other side of the water during your water baptism (or was lifted out of that grave like Jesus by God's Spirit), so the Spirit of God in you will raise your body on the other side of your real grave in the earth. You do not have to fear death. No! Believers must know on their dying beds and in their last moments: "Even though I walk through the valley of the shadow of death, I will fear no evil, for you are with me; your rod and your staff, they comfort me (Ps 23:4, ESVUK)." You already followed exactly the same path of death during your water baptism. You were already raised prophetically when God's Spirit lifted you out of that water that you had to go through on His command. God was with you the whole time and specifically at that precise moment, you went into that water. Now you can rest in the prophetic. It will again be 100 % the same! You can just rest and let go. Stay in the peace of this memory that God gave to us as His church of believers in His enormous Grace and in His Unending Love. Your loved ones in Christ around you saw you go into that water grave during your water baptism, but they also saw how you came out of the water in the New Life of Christ that is predestined for believers on the other side. The thought will give them rest and assurance that all was well with your soul after your physical death, because they know what you proclaimed with your baptism. I promise you in the Name of Jesus Christ, the Name above all other names, the loved ones that will see your earthly death, will definitely also see your resurrection in Christ one day! This time the celebration will be thousand times more glorious than the day you came out of that water during your water baptism! Glory to the Most High God forever!

Day 38 Born into an infinitely bigger Realm or Heavenly Kingdom

You and I were living in a very small world or space inside our mothers' wombs. Then one day her water broke and we came out of it into a completely new world. We can never go back to that old small space again, even though it did have an essential purpose in preparing us and getting us ready for our birth. It is impossible to go back, because we have been born in a new space infinitely bigger than the small space or the limited world where we used to live in. The birth made all the difference. We are now free to live and to move freely in the bigger realm (compared to the limited space we used to have). Some parents decided that they do not want their little children to enter the new or bigger world for purposes of their own name, so they simply murdered them inside the womb. Another name for the legal murders of infants that the worldly system promote is called "abortion". You can then murder as many kids as you want to with the law on your side and without being legally responsible for it to other people in this earthly realm. Those poor little children never got the opportunity to live and to be part of a much bigger realm than the one they experienced. Some died naturally inside the womb in spite of the fact that their parents desired them to join them in the bigger realm, because this current earth is still experiencing the curse of vanity, until the Kingdom of Christ will manifest in the New Earth.

Just like the above mentioned, the coming out of that water grave during our baptism reminds us of an infinitely bigger Spirit Realm into which we were born in Spirit during our spiritual birth (compared to the limited earthly realm). The chief governor (Acts 8:27, GNV) could also armed his mind like that during his baptism. "When they came up out of the water, the Lord's Spirit suddenly took Philip away. The eunuch never saw him again but went on his way rejoicing (Acts 8:39, CEB)." Just like that, "As soon as Yeshua had been immersed, he came up out of the water. At that moment heaven was opened, he saw the Spirit of God coming down upon him like a dove (Matthew 3:16, CJB)." You will not see, walk, enter the open heavens, or experience the Spirit of God, *unless you are born again or born from Above* (John 3:3). The baptism reminds you of the fact that you were an earthly citizen because you were born in it. The baptism will also remind you that you can only become a family member of Christ or part of the family of our King (or Heaven) by being born from Him or by being born from Above. There is no other Way! Only One Way and His name is Jesus.

Day 39 Without A Past!

A small newborn baby has no past! There is a division of water between the old and the new (like Noah and the Israelites on the other side of the water). Noah could not go back through the water. The Israelites could not go back through the water. A small baby cannot go back to his previous residence inside his mother's womb. You and I that tasted the rebirth cannot go back to our past. You can arm your mind or soul with the same thought that you have no evil or corrupt past, but just a future in the Kingdom of Christ into which you were born.

If a baby is arrested, directly after his birth for something, he did in his "past" or the place he came from, we will definitely know the people who arrested him are completely insane. Just like that, you must not allow anybody to try to find all kinds of curses or bloodline curses or an evil past in your natural bloodline after you have been born again. People, who try to do that, despise the cross of Jesus and the new birth. You are a total new creation in His Kingdom thanks to that birthing.

"When anyone is in Christ, it is a whole new world. The old things are gone; suddenly, everything is new! (2 Cor 5:17, ERV)." You are born into the Royal family of His Royal Majesty Jesus Christ the King of all kings and the Lord of all lords. You have only His spotless past, His shining presence and His Glorious Future ahead of you. Whenever somebody tells you that you are poor due to things your parents did, or that your grandmother was a witch and therefore God hates you for what they did, just realize that they do not understand the rebirth or any birth for that matter. It is demon talk. Recognize it for what it is. I have seen many women who try to do deliverance by always discovering new evils in others' lives and pasts. They may love Jesus, but they are enemies of the cross and despise it. We met so many of them constantly studying new roots of evil, but we have never seen one of them that are free. Only Christ and the cross can free you from the old! Remember what Scripture is saying: "The Father has delivered and drawn us to Himself out of the control and the dominion of darkness and has transferred us into the kingdom of the Son of His love (Col 1:13, AMPC)."

We have been transferred out of the dominion of darkness. We are now in a total new location namely the Kingdom of Christ. You died for your past and your previous bloodline. You were born into a new Royal bloodline. Do not let anybody rob you from and distract you from the Truth. Your baptism confirms the Truth!

Day 40 Baptism is to remind you of a new birth

Do not be part of the group that Peter warned against. He said: "For they willingly forget [the fact] that the heavens existed long ago by the word of God, and the earth was formed out of water and by water (2 Peter 3:5, Amplified)."

God's Spirit baptized this current earth when God took it out of that water (Gen 1:2, 3). This was after the Ice Age (like scientists called it). The first message in the Bible is therefore the message of the baptism or Life out of death. The present earth came into existence and growth could take place on it after it was taken out of the water. It was in "fetus" or only "in potential" form inside the water, but in order to reach its predestined purpose, God had to bring it into its rightful place and therefore He took it out of that water. The Creator was like a medical doctor or midwife that brought the current earth into existence. He saw and formed its changes after its birthing. Coming out of water is always associated with new life and people know it in their spirits. This is why even the atheistic evolutionists believe it, agree with the Bible and preach that life came out of water. Noah experienced the "new earth" that was "born" after the flood destroyed the demonic beings and giants of Genesis 6:2, 4, and 6. The Israelites also experienced freedom from Egypt and from Pharaoh after they went through the water (just like Noah). They could not return, but they could still miss the fullness that God planned for them in the Promised Land or in His Kingdom.

It is not just about being saved for us. There is so much more than just the concept of heaven and hell. The murderer on the cross was saved, but he never experienced the joy of walking on the other side of the water with Jesus on this earth and growing to adulthood or maturity in spirit. He was saved, but he had no works that followed him (Rom 2:6, 10, Matt 10:42, 1 Cor 5:10, Eph 1:18, John 8:39, Col 3:23, 24, 1 Pet 1:4, 5, Gal 6:9, 1 Tim 6:17-19, Heb 6:10-12 etc.). Now is our time to intimately walk with Him and show Him our hunger for more of Him. You will surely get what you want or what your heart desire! It is a promise in His Name! Those that desire His presence will be rewarded with Him or with His presence!

Day 41 The world is crucified unto me, and I unto the world.

It was a habit for those people in John's time and in the time of the disciples of the Bible to walk into the Jordan River from the far side of Jerusalem. John or Jesus's disciples would then once baptize or immerse the people in the Jordan river, because there was enough water to baptize them in and according to the command that John got from God (John 3:22, 23, Acts 8:36-40). The person being baptized could experience, think and know that it is impossible for Him or her to breath under water or continue to exist in a grave. It was like a water grave. It reminded them of the death that they died for the present world by being buried like that. Because of their baptism or immersion, they could make that connection in their minds with the death of Jesus their Savior on the cross and His and their own burial. They could think of His and their own resurrection when coming out of that water. They would then exit the river on the side of Jerusalem and walk in the direction of Jerusalem as symbolic of the direction of their new lives. It was symbolic of leaving their old lives behind in that water grave and symbolic of the total new Life that they would then live.

"And those who belong to Christ Jesus (the Messiah) have crucified the flesh (the godless human nature) with its passions and appetites and desires (Gal 5:24, AMPC)." "But God forbid that I should glory, save in the cross of our Lord Jesus Christ, by whom the world is crucified unto me, and I unto the world (Gal 6:14, BRG)." Yes, there is now a division between you and the old earth in spirit. Scripture is very clear about it. You died for it. The world with its sinful lusts and desires lost you and you are lost for this world in order to live in the New Life that God has for us!

Day 42 Jonah was once baptized in the sea

Jonah told the people that the sea would calm if they would throw him overboard (Jonah 1:12). The people did that. They killed Jonah by throwing him overboard (Jonah 1:15). They most likely saw his death. They probably saw how the fish swallowed him, because the typology of God is always perfect (like the marriage between one man and one woman that are able to become one without perversion – just like God ordained it to be). The sea then got calm due to his death (Jonah 1:16). Jonah was still alive when he reached the stomach of the fish because he was still praying his last prayers from there (Jonah 2:1). Jonah died because nobody can live inside the stomach of a fish. It can be seen in Scripture: "I cried in mine affliction unto the Lord, and he heard me: out of the belly of hell cried I, and thou heardest my voice (Jonah 2:2, GNV)." "From deep in the world of the dead I cried for help, and you heard me (Jonah 2:2, GNT)." "From the depths of death I called (Jonah 2:2, TLB)." Most translations say that he cried from "Sheol" (hell). "I sank to the foundations of the mountains; the earth with its prison bars closed behind me forever! But You raised my life from the Pit, Lord my God! (Jonah 2:6, HCSB)." God heard Jonah's prayer. He commanded the fish to spit Jonah out. Jonah died when his body was three days and three nights inside that fish. He was resurrected on the third day by the Word of God and again walked the earth. He preached and could be seen and heard.

Jonah was baptized in short, because he died once during his baptism and God's Spirit rose Him from that death. After his baptism, he preached so powerful that the whole city of Nineveh came to Christ! They saw the living evidence of life after death or the resurrection power of God in Jonah's baptism! This was no coincidence, because Jesus also ministered powerfully after His water baptism. The Jonah sign is perfect! There is none like our Sovereign God and Savior Jesus Christ who has power over both death and Life!

Day 43 In His Grace He gave the unbelievers a sign on their request.

Jesus did incredible miracles, but still the people did not believe Him or in Him. In their eyes, He was making use of demonic powers. The religious world is still on that track. They criticize the real prophets of God in their own religious weakness and always rob God from His Glory (Mat 12:24, Mark 3:22). They could not realize that the One Person in front of them was the One God or One Spirit God of the Universe, but just in flesh and blood form. Still they wanted more miracles and more signs and asked Him for it (Matt 12:38). Jesus could do another 200 million miracles, but unbelievers will always connect it to the devil and quote Scripture for that, instead of seeing Jesus in it and believing in Him.

Jesus is always gracious and even though He spoke against their unbelief (Matt 12:38), He wanted to silence everybody's unbelief forever with a sign from heaven that would touch and make all people believe throughout all generations and for all eternity. The only sign that all people would get, was the sign of Jonah (Matt 12:49, 16:4). Jonah was three days and three nights in the fish (Jonah 1:17). "In the same way that Jonah spent three days and nights in the big fish, so will the Son of Man spend three days and nights in the depths of the earth (Matt 12:40, GNT)." The same God that orchestrated the prophetic sign of Jonah stood in flesh and blood form on this earth. He told the people on more than one occasion before His death, that they would again see the sign of Jonah, but this time it will not be a fish, but a grave in which His body would be. The sign of Jonah happened with precise detail in Jesus. It will be the only sign to all unbelievers and atheists all over the world in order to convince them of His Royal Majesty King Jesus the King of all kings! This is the one sign that will change your own life forever and the lives of all other people on earth namely the real baptism of Jesus that happened at Calvary (Luke 12:50). Tell me, how can you ever doubt? Can you see the sign of death and Life!

Day 44 Baptized in Him.

Fish and fishes in the Bible represent humanity. I already explained that Jesus became Man forever. It is not coincidence that He used bread and fish. He broke it and distributed it among His followers. Both the broken bread and the broken fish were pointing to His own body that would be broken for us. If you can see it and believe it, the sign of Jonah or his baptism will have even more meaning to you. The Bible is clear about the fact that we died with Christ (Gal 2:20, Rom 6:4-11). We believe that Jesus died because God said so and Scripture is clear about it. Scripture is just as clear about the fact that we died with Christ. God said it and that settled it. Just as sure as He died, we died in God's mind and estimation. Just as sure as Jesus was raised from the death, we were also raised from the death. "God loved us so much that he made us alive with Christ. God raised us from death to life with Christ Jesus, and he has given us a place beside Christ in heaven (Eph 2:5, 6, CEV)." Believe Scripture. "The word [is] faithful; for if we have died together with [him], we shall also live together (2 Tim 2:11, Darby)." No doubt! The Big Fish swallowed Jonah as a prophetic image of us being in Christ. Jonah was in Christ. "For in Him we live and move and have our being (Acts 17:28, BSB)." Jonah died *in Him* (Col 2:20), but was also raised *in Him* and with Him (Gal 2:20). When He went down to the depths of Sheol, we were in Him (Rom 10:7). When He was raised to the right hand side of God, we were still in Him and we still are at this very moment. His baptism was our baptism! You were not alone during your baptism, but in Him. His Life is now our Life. He is our Energy. He is our only Source and our very Existence! There is none besides Him.

Day 45 No coincidence. Predestination!

The baptism of Jonah or the sign of Jonah is very clear and very strong. Jonah knew that the sea could only calm if he as the scapegoat would be killed. We already explained how the sea represents the nations in their fleshly turmoil. Jesus had to die, because there could be no Peace for humanity without their sins being paid for. Jesus was the Lamb of God. No other sacrifice could ever end the turmoil of the nations. Jesus died and His death and resurrection brought the Kingdom of God's Peace to this earth.

Like Jonah who was baptized by one single immersion, Jesus also only died once for the sin of the whole world. It is not necessary for Him to come and die for a third time or a seventh time. He died once only. You also die once in Him only and after that, you can start to live from the Eternal Life within you.

Jonah was raised on the third day. Jesus often prophesied that He would die and rise on the third day. He did this even long before His actual death. Jesus said: 'Saying: The Son of man must suffer many things, and be rejected by the ancients and chief priests and scribes, and be killed, and the third day rise again (Luke 9:22, DRA)." Jesus knew that He was Reality or the Objective Truth revealed and that Jonah was only a shadow type pointing to Him (Luke 11:29). "And while they are living in Galilee, Jesus said to them, 'The Son of Man is about to be delivered up to the hands of men, and they shall kill him, and the third day he shall rise,' and they were exceeding sorry (Matthew 17:22-23, Young's Literal Translation)."

He told them He would rise. This sign is also prophetic of our own resurrection that will soon be seen in manifested glory when the sons of God are going to be revealed (Rom. 8:18-30). His manifested Glory will flood the earth and the seas or nations will be calmed.

Day 46 Baptism proclaims His Grace.

"I called out to the Lord in my distress, and he answered me. From the belly of the underworld I cried out for help; you have heard my voice (Jonah 2:2, CEB)." "Out of the belly of hell cried I, and thou heardest my voice (Jonah 2:2, GNV)." What Jonah experienced was terrifying! "I sank to the foundations of the mountains; the earth with its prison bars closed behind me *forever*! But You raised my life from the Pit, Lord my God (Jonah 2:6, HCSB)!" Jonah could literally experience how the prison bars of the pit in the earth closed him in. Just think of the terror that he experienced when he realized it was forever! He begged God to free him and to give him a second chance (Grace), and God did. God took him from the pit and rose him to heavenly places with Him. It was all *Grace*! God could have left Jonah there as eternal punishment for his rebellion, disobedience and the sin of fleeing from God, but God gave him a second chance in His marvelous *Grace* and Mercy.

The baptism of Jonah is the revelation of the greatest Mercy ever shown in the universe and reveals the magnitude of God's Love. Your own baptism is also about the second chance that God is giving you. You sinned and you deserved death, but God did not keep it against you and will not ever keep it against you. Instead of leaving us in hell where we deserve to be, He took us from the lowest level of existence possible and exalted us to the highest possible rank and level with Him in heavenly places as blood family. Your baptism proclaim His Eternal and His marvelous Grace. It is grace. It is all about Grace. "I once was lost, but now I'm found!" What a God. Such unending Grace, Eternal Mercy, Compassion without end and Love without measure!

Without Him, we are lost!

Day 47 Walk in Grace.

After your rebirth and your proclamation of accepting His Grace to all powers in heaven, on earth and under the earth with your baptism, you can daily and consciously know that each step, each breath that you take, each heartbeat and each blink of your eye is just pure Grace out of God's Hands. If God could lift you from the gutter most to the Uttermost, why can other people not experience, learn and taste the same Grace? Jonah had to learn this lesson.

God send Jonah to Nineveh, but he did not want to go, because Nineveh was the capital city of Assyria and not part of Israel according to his OT thought pattern. Racism is reality in a life before the cross and young carnal Christians. Assyria was not Israel's friend. The Israelites thought that God only worked with them and never realized that He also cared for all the other nations and other people all over the globe. Jonah was a racist in short. He did not want to go, but after his death and resurrection, baptism or experience with the fish, he finally went to Nineveh against his own will. He told the city that God was going to destroy them, because they do not acknowledge Him and lived and behaved like animals. The whole city repented. God was satisfied. The God of Grace decided to spare them. Jonah was extremely angry and said to God that he did not want to go to Nineveh in the first place, because "I knew you're a compassionate God, slow to anger, overflowing with gracious love, and reluctant to send trouble (Jonah 4:2, ISV)." He blamed God for forgiving people so easily and for His tremendous Grace. He was glad that God saved him when he cried out to God from the pit of the earth, but he got angry when God shows mercy and grace to other people that he thought do not deserve God's mercy and favor. Are we not often the same?

Jonah wanted to see the city being destroyed by God in order to maintain his reputation as a powerful prophet. Then God made a plant grow miraculously quick and it provided shade for Jonah. Jonah was very happy with the nice cool shadow. God then send a worm that killed the plant. Again, Jonah was angry.

God then talked to Jonah. God told him that it is unfair of him to want the plant that only took one night to grow to stay alive, but then on the other hand think that God is unfair because He does not want to wipe out the people from the city of Nineveh that He loved and cared for over many years.

Oh, how we must have compassion, church. Let us love people and care for them because of who we are on this side of the cross. What you have and experience today on this earth, is pure *Grace*. Do not expect God to only be nice and good to you only, your family or your tribe or your nation and not to other people as well. No! God so loved the world that He died for each person on this earth. Let us continue to reach out with God's Grace to even the wicked on earth. If He did it for me, He can surely do it for them!

Day 48 The two legs of your baptism: "My part and His part".

"But you cannot see my face. No one can see me and continue to live (Ex 33:20, ERV)."
God is Spirit (John 4:24). Living people cannot see Spirit, but we know that there is a Bigger Realm or Great Person or Great Spirit behind this physical earth. He is holy or the only Holy Spirit controlling everything in the universe. No other person can be holy out of him or herself. We desperately need Him and His Life in us in order to be holy. John saw Christ in His Glory. "When I saw him, I fell at his feet like a dead man. But he put his right hand on me and said, "Do not be afraid. I am the First and the Last." (Rev. 1:17, NCV). When you really see God, you will definitely realize how weak you are in your own strength. One thought will overwhelm you: "I am nothing in myself". Only One deserve the Glory. You will fall down like a dead person in front of Christ in His holiness. That is our part. We must reckon ourselves dead to sin and dead to this world or dead to anything that can rob us from God's glory.

Christ will then raise you by His mighty and powerful Word. Ezekiel experienced the same. "The appearance of the radiant light resembled that of a rainbow shining in a cloud on a rainy day. This was what the appearance of the form of the glory of the Lord resembled. When I saw all of this, I fell flat on my face. Then I heard a voice speaking. "Son of Man," the Lord said, "get up on your feet. I want to talk to you." Even while he was speaking to me, the Spirit entered me, set me on my feet, and I listened to the voice that had been speaking to me (Ezek 1:28, 2:1-2, ISV)." Do not exalt yourself. It is not your job. Our task is to humble ourselves before the Mighty God of the Universe. If we do, He will lift us up and let us stand and walk by the power of His Mighty Word or Spirit! "Can you remember the song: "Humble yourselves in the sight of the Lord, and He will lift you up…?" That is trust. Trust is to not try to attain a position or status for yourself out of your own might and own power!

Day 49   Trust God the way Jonah did!

After I studied law, I was public prosecutor and worked under an extremely difficult man. The main magistrate and head of the office did not get angry. No! He was angry! He communicated in an extremely aggressive way to people, was always frustrated and nobody could ever live up to his expectations. Everybody in the office was unhappy. People feared him and nobody had any respect for him.

God spoke to me. I realized that I had to be a Jonah. "Jonah told them, "Throw me into the sea, and it will calm down (Jonah 1:12, Amplified)." There was an opportunity for me to stay on in this job, but I decided to go and face the boss. I made and appointment with him and gently told him in his face how everybody experienced him (including myself). It is always difficult to try to make people see the difference between leadership and manipulation and intimidation. Nevertheless, I then left after that and left my colleagues behind in an improved atmosphere.

We all have blind spots. "You don't know what you don't know". That is why we need honest people around us to help us in truth (even if it hurts our ego). You need your husband's or your wife's opinion. I also had to be a Jonah on other occasions where my reputation and my provision were involved and at those times, God granted me the Grace to choose His will and not my own.

I admire Jonah. He completely trusted God with his life even if it meant to be thrown overboard in the ocean far from land and far from any other safety that can be seen and on top of that in stormy conditions. Sometimes I just honestly pray from my heart to have Jonah's trust and faith in God, because I want to be gently lowered onto a lifeboat in calm and pleasant conditions near a definite Island that I can see or near another boat that can maybe save me! What more can I say?

Day 50 Sevenfold increase in the tempo of revelation.

God progressively reveals Truth and is busy restoring His church. The church is busy increasing in strength, Light and Glory. First, it was pitch-dark night, and then Luther received the first restorative Light. It was about Faith as the only substance necessary to save us (and not all those dead works). Then the Anabaptists received more light from God regarding the baptism. The Cloud moved from where Luther was. We must always move with Him (the Cloud).

God gave me a dream over this weekend. Father showed me how technology and the tempo that in which new things are patented and developed increased over the years. The one discovery leads to the next and it is just continuing to increase in speed and momentum. My earthly dad, who died long ago, was also in my dream. He showed me some remarkable discoveries in the transport industry and in the area of communication that are going to come. Then God spoke and said: "The growth and increase in knowledge that you see in the technological area, is similar to the increase of my knowledge and Truth that I progressively reveal to my children." I could see testimonies of several people being filmed. I saw a movie with the combined testimonies of several people simultaneously in it that struck people's hearts (even famous people from sport circles). I saw more camps that are Christian and unity, honor and respect for each other and love. I could literally see how Christians are moving closer to each other. Even where projects started in opposite directions, the people started to find each other in Him and all got excited about His Kingdom. God then spoke loud and clear for me to hear and He said that the tempo of new revelation that will reach His church would increase sevenfold. I was so excited. The time between sow and harvest are getting shorter and shorter (just like the tempo of new technology being invented gets shorter and shorter). The Glory of the Rock (Jesus Christ) will fill the earth. Those with opened eyes will see and experience the increasing Glory of our Lord Jesus Christ!

In order to enable even the children to understand the (baptizō) or baptism of Jesus, I decided to place a link to an anime. Enjoy. It is less than 2 minutes.
https://www.youtube.com/watch?v=lMzlB185JSc

I know it was cruel. The world still does not have any time or hospitality for any citizens of heaven. It is different for the people of the Kingdom. People come to us in hostility, but we treat them and accept them as royalty due to this tremendous price that was paid also for them!

EPILOGUE:

I want to thank you out of my heart for reading this book. I thank you for the time and effort that you were willing to sacrifice in order to do that. May God richly bless you.

"So we have not stopped praying for you since we first heard about you. We ask God to give you complete knowledge of his will and to give you spiritual wisdom and understanding. Then the way you live will always honor and please the Lord, and your lives will produce every kind of good fruit. All the while, you will grow as you learn to know God better and better. We also pray that you will be strengthened with all his glorious power so you will have all the endurance and patience you need. May you be filled with joy, always thanking the Father. He has enabled you to share in the inheritance that belongs to his people, who live in the light. For he has rescued us from the kingdom of darkness and transferred us into the Kingdom of his dear Son, who purchased our freedom and forgave our sins.

Christ Is Supreme. Christ is the visible image of the invisible God. He existed before anything was created and is supreme over all creation, for through him God created everything in the heavenly realms and on earth. He made the things we can see and the things we can't see - such as thrones, kingdoms, rulers, and authorities in the unseen world. Everything was created through him and for him. He existed before anything else, and he holds all creation together. Christ is also the head of the church, which is his body. He is the beginning, supreme over all who rise from the dead. So he is first in everything. For God in all his fullness was pleased to live in Christ, and through him God reconciled everything to himself. He made peace with everything in heaven and on earth by means of Christ's blood on the cross.

This includes you who were once far away from God. You were his enemies, separated from him by your evil thoughts and actions. Yet now he has reconciled you to himself through the death of Christ in his physical body. As a result, he has brought you into his own presence, and you are holy and blameless as you stand before him without a single fault. But you must continue to believe this truth and stand firmly in it. Don't drift away from the assurance you received when you heard the Good News." (Col 1:9-23, NLT).

Be blessed! (And do not forget to read "The Unintended Book of Grace")
Thanks
JJ

Christ's Grace And Baptism

www.ingramcontent.com/pod-product-compliance
Lightning Source LLC
Chambersburg PA
CBHW052102110526
44591CB00013B/2311